The Caught Habits
of Language

William Sydney Graham (1918–1986) was born in Greenock, Scotland, and trained as an engineer. He settled in west Cornwall where a growing colony of experimental artists came to respect the determination and acute self-criticism with which he pursued his poetry. In 1949 T.S. Eliot adopted his work, and Faber and Faber remain his primary publisher. Key works are *New Collected Poems* (Faber and Faber, 2004) and *The Nightfisherman: Selected Letters of W.S. Graham* (Carcanet Press, 1999).

Rachael Boast was born in Suffolk in 1975 and is the author of three collections of poetry, most recently *Void Studies* (Picador, 2016). She is co-editor of *The Echoing Gallery: Bristol Poets and Art in the City* (Redcliffe Press, 2013).

Andy Ching was born in Glasgow in 1965 and lives in Bristol. He is co-founder and Managing Editor of Donut Press.

Nathan Hamilton is a poet and publisher. He is co-founder and Managing Director/Editor of UEA Publishing Project Ltd. He edited *Dear World & Everyone In It* (Bloodaxe Books, 2013).

Jeremy Noel-Tod teaches in the School of Literature, Drama and Creative Writing at the University of East Anglia. His publications as an editor include *The Oxford Companion to Modern Poetry* (Oxford University Press, 2013) and R.F. Langley's *Complete Poems* (Carcanet Press, 2015).

The Caught Habits of Language

An Entertainment for W.S. Graham
for Him Having Reached One Hundred

Edited by Rachael Boast, Andy Ching
and Nathan Hamilton

With an introduction by Jeremy Noel-Tod

Donut Press

Donut Press, Flat 1, The Pump House,
Pump House Lane, Bristol, BS4 4RQ

Published by Donut Press in 2018

ISBN: 9780956644589

Designed and typeset by Liam Relph
Printed and bound by T.J. International Ltd, Padstow

The Caught Habits of Language is published as part of
Language is Where the People Are: W.S. Graham at One Hundred.

Donut Press acknowledges Creative Scotland for financial assistance
from the National Lottery.

T.T.B.B.

I say this silence or, better, construct this space
So that somehow something may move across
The caught habits of language to you and me

'The Constructed Space', W.S. Graham

Editors' Acknowledgements

Thanks are sent to all contributors, and those who kindly offered poems for inclusion. We would also like to thank Creative Scotland for providing financial support from the National Lottery, and the Estates of Nessie Dunsmuir, W.S. Graham and Michael Seward Snow for allowing us to reproduce materials for which they hold copyright.

We are grateful to the University of East Anglia for research support that allowed Nathan Hamilton and David Nowell Smith to visit key W.S. Graham archives, and to UEA Publishing Project Ltd for further support. We thank Justin Snow for his kindness, A.B. Jackson for editorial assistance, David Nowell Smith for his research contribution and Nicola Kegode for applying her palaeographic skills to the manuscript of W.S. Graham's poem 'An Entertainment for W.S. Graham for Him Having Reached Sixty-five'.

A small selection of the W.S. Graham poems included in this anthology were first published in a special feature on the author in *Poetry* (January 2018). We would like to thank Holly Amos, Lindsay Garbutt, Fred Sasaki and Don Share for their work in developing the feature; further acknowledgement is due to Don and Christian Wiman, co-editors of the anthology *The Open Door: One Hundred Poems, One Hundred Years of Poetry Magazine* (University of Chicago Press, 2012), upon which aspects of *The Caught Habits of Language* were modelled.

We are grateful to W.S. Graham's friends and publishers who, together with a number of scholars, have helped to ensure Graham's poetry remains visible and increasingly admired.

Finally, thank you Rosalind and Pia Mudaliar, Mike, Jago and Kofi Bruce, for your company and hospitality, help and support.

List of Illustrations

Contents

Notes

Contributors and Acknowledgements

Source notes for poems by W.S. Graham

W.S. Graham bibliography

Introduction

'Thoughts on the making of poetry are often the subject of my own poems' W.S. Graham, 1970

'The poem, to you, is, of course, what its words compel you to make of it' W.S. Graham, 1949

What should we make of W.S. Graham? The answer that this anthology offers is: much. The breadth and warmth of the tributes to Graham collected here are testament to his achievement as a poet whose words can still be heard – in his own characteristic phrase – 'speaking towards' our time.

'The poet or painter steers his life to maim / Himself somehow for the job', Graham wrote in 'The Thermal Stair', his elegy for the painter, Peter Lanyon, who died following a gliding accident:

> …His job is Love
> Imagined into words or paint to make
> An object that will stand and will not move.

'To make' was the single-minded aim of Graham's gently maimed life. Although he only published seven collections of verse over thirty-five years, archival research is beginning to uncover how much work went into perfecting each poetic 'object' at his 'untidy dreadful table' (now in the Scottish Poetry Library), its wood diagrammed with knife scratches and crowded with worm-like cigarette burns. Writing poetry was, Graham said, when he felt 'most alive', but it was also hard labour – made harder by the fact that his dedication went largely unrewarded and little celebrated in his lifetime. Yet he seems to have worked in the belief (as have many of the most original poets) that his poetry was as much for the future as the present: he was 'the labourer carrying the bricks of his time and on the scaffolding of an unknown construction'. As the selection of previously unpublished pieces made by the editors of this anthology shows, Graham was fastidiously discriminating about what he allowed to leave the dreadful table into tidy print. Convened for his centenary year, this gathering of eighty poets represents some of the backdated wages of fame.

William Sydney Graham ('I answer to Sydney') was born a week and a day after the end of the First World War at 1 Hope Street, Greenock, Scotland. This 'rivetting town', as he later called it, on the bank of the river Clyde, was dominated by shipbuilding. Graham's father worked as an engineer, while his mother was a shopkeeper. After leaving school at fourteen, he was apprenticed as a draughtsman in an engineering firm and studied structural engineering in Glasgow. In 1938, a bursary enabled him to study literature and philosophy for a year at Newbattle Abbey, an adult education college near Edinburgh. It was there that he met Nessie Dunsmuir, who would later become his wife. During the Second World War, having been diagnosed with an ulcer and declared unfit for service, he worked for a time in a torpedo factory in Scotland and then as a school teacher. Living among artists, writers and refugees in Glasgow, he began to publish his poetry. His first collection, *Cage without Grievance* (1942) was followed by a sequence in the Poetry Scotland series, *The Seven Journeys* (1944).

In 1943, Graham and a colleague, Mary Harris, left their teaching jobs and travelled five hundred miles south to live in a pair of caravans near the village of Germoe in Cornwall. The relationship did not last, however, and in 1944 Harris returned to Scotland to give birth to their daughter, Rosalind. Graham was then joined at the caravans by Nessie, and saw out the war in Cornwall, living off the land and writing his next collection, *2ND Poems* (1945 – he later said that the title was also an abbreviation of 'To Nessie Dunsmuir'). He went on to spend time in America and Europe before returning to the Cornish coast, again with Nessie, whom he married in 1954, the year before the book publication of his long poem and masterpiece, *The Nightfishing*. In 1956, they settled in an old coastguard's cottage on the Atlantic promontory of Gurnard's Head, where they subsisted on little money and no electricity. Living near St Ives, Graham made important friendships with artists who had been drawn to the area, including Peter Lanyon, Bryan Wynter and Roger Hilton. In 1967, the Grahams moved to 4 Mount View, Madron, the small terrace house where Graham would live until his death from cancer on 9th January 1986. During his last decade Graham increasingly felt the effects of a lifetime of drinking and penury, but also enjoyed his greatest fame: a *Collected Poems* appeared in 1979, and he returned to Scotland for the first time since the 1950s to give readings from his work.

Graham's enduring affection for his place of birth informs a number of his poems. The Firth of Clyde landscape around Loch Long and Loch Thom was his own 'long loch of memory', and in later life he yearned to return. He was friendly with other Scottish poets, such as Edwin Morgan and Hugh MacDiarmid, but he chose to keep his distance from what he saw as 'the selfconsciousness of the Scottish art scene'. By settling among the working villages of the far south-west of England, however, Graham also kept his distance from literary London. Writing to Morgan in 1950, he described the Land's End peninsula as 'early and Celtic and definitely unEnglish'. It had also been little evoked in verse, and Graham was gratified when, in 1984, the Cornish journalist Frank Ruhrmund referred to the area around Gurnard's Head as 'Graham country'.

As a poet, Graham developed an original voice that drew on the long vernacular history of verse in Britain. He celebrates that ancestry in the dark nonsense-poem, 'The Answerers', which alludes to Scots poems and ballads, including that of Sir Patrick Spens, who is commanded to undertake a sea-voyage so dangerous that 'the tear blinded his ee'. Always drawn to the figure of the lone adventurer, during his last illness Graham drafted an extraordinarily raw and stoical meditation, '[It is as Though the Very Movement Comes Out of Silence]', which imagines stepping out of the 'cancer threshold pain / […] I can't tell you about', and instead putting on his poet's 'coat' to walk the 'empty night-road' of the blank page. Typically for Graham's late work, the verse feels its way into being doubtfully ('I walk in braille'). But when it ends with the couplet 'On my cheek / The western rain gives my cheek a lick', the poem arrives at a joyful calling back to the unknown English lyricist who sang, in the sixteenth century or before,

> Western wind when wilt thou blow
> The small rain down can rain
> Christ if my love were in my arms
> And I in my bed again

A notebook from 1949, the year in which he published his fourth collection, *The White Threshold*, gives an insight into how Graham very deliberately apprenticed himself to be a poet – or, to use the Scots term, a makar – in the modernist tradition he admired. In between reflections on his own writing, he copied out passages from T.S. Eliot, who had recently, as poetry editor at Faber and Faber, become his publisher. Graham remembered this life-changing event in 'The Night City', a poem about London: 'I found Eliot and he said yes // And sprang into a Holmes cab' – lines that suggest, with their allusion to Arthur Conan Doyle's great detective, the legendary aura that surrounded the author of *The Waste Land* and *Four Quartets* in the late 1940s. This is also something he comments on in his 1949 notebook:

> Eliot – the legend behind the man making his poetry 'magic'.
>   each profundity of technique put forwards charges
>   the poetry more.
>   The constructing of the Magician

Later, he returns to this idea with a command to self:

> In future projects – remember the constructing of the myth – the feel
> of the 'magic' texture overall – of the poetry connected with Graham.

'To construct' was a magical verb in Graham's poetry of making. In the notebook he speculates that a poem is 'a created space, a constructed solitude'. Nine years later, this became the conceit of an 'abstract' poem, 'The Constructed Space', addressed to the unknown reader:

> I say this silence or, better, construct this space
> So that somehow something may move across
> The caught habits of language to you and me.

Here is Graham the stage magician, showing his hands empty to the audience, and then producing 'something' – a poem – out of the thin air of speech. The caught habit is the conjurer's rabbit: something real and alive that the poem has put before our very eyes. Elsewhere he called it 'The Beast in the Space': an imaginary animal, caged in words, which 'pads and sniffs between us'.

The only critical essay that Graham ever published, 'Notes on a Poetry of Release' (1946), contains two important and related statements: 'a poem is to be a successful construction of words' and 'the shape of all of us in this language'. The 'release' in question is whatever the poem unlocks in the reader: 'the poem itself is dumb' but 'can be used by the reader to find out something about himself'. Although the experience is necessarily private and individual ('the poem is not a handing out of the same packet to everyone'), Graham's vision of poetry is emphatically collective. Both halves of the essay end with the same sentiment, almost verbatim, like a refrain:

> It is a good direction to believe that this language which is so scored and impressed by the commotion of us all since its birth can be arranged to in its turn impress significantly for the good of each individual. Let us endure the sudden affection of the language.

Graham's poems – which are often nocturnes – speak repeatedly out of the silence and solitude that he saw as their necessary condition ('On this side of the words it's late'). But their raw material, the words, were gathered out of 'the commotion of us all'. In the pubs that he loved to inhabit, he was, he said, 'the man of technique who books the phrases of drinking and affection so that later I might explore the mechanics of their memorableness and vitality'.

In one poem, 'Enter a Cloud', we can observe this sobering process happening in real time. Part 1 introduces us to the poet lying on Zennor Hill in Cornwall one afternoon, 'in a bower of bramble / Into which I have fallen'. The clumsiness of the accident and the topsy-turvy explanation gives us a clue to what is really going on. Graham liked to drink in the The Tinners Arms in

Zennor, a village that lay several miles from his home in Madron. On the way home, Zennor Hill and its brambles have got in the way (a similar mishap seems to be recalled in '[And Who Will Hold Me in the Dark]'). And so a poem begins, as the poet watches a cumulonimbus cloud crossing the blue sky: 'an elongated white anvil is sailing / Not wanting to be a symbol'.

It is tempting to the poet – and the critic – to see the lone cloud as a mythological symbol of creative power, a sky-anvil on which a poem can be hammered out (he has already seen the sea as a 'table-top'). But rather than co-opt it in this lonely way, the drowsy speaker starts to 'disintegrate' and become a cloud himself, floating imaginatively through the lives of friends elsewhere: 'Jean in London' and 'Albert Strick' in Madron, who is 'teeling / Broccoli for the winter'. Raising himself out of the bracken as the cloud disappears, the poet takes a comically tipsy bow to his readers ('Thank you. And for your applause.'), before going on to thank 'the real ones / Who have made this possible': the cloud, the place names, the people, 'and good words like brambles, / Bower, spiked, fox, anvil, teeling'.

Graham's acknowledgement of how reality resists the romantic symbol-seeker goes to the heart of his later poetry, as collected in *Malcolm Mooney's Land* (1970) and *Implements in Their Places* (1977), as well as the posthumous volumes, *Uncollected Poems* (1990) and *Aimed at Nobody* (1993). In these books he achieved the wish expressed in his 1949 notebook: an oeuvre of magical charm. Graham himself defended his earlier work against the critical narrative of progression, arguing to one correspondent that

> My early poems are as good as my later poems. They are maybe not as fashionable, but neither are my later poems. The early poems are other objects with their own particular energies. To say I am getting better, or have written myself into a greater clearness, is very much a surface observation.

Readers, nevertheless, continue to respond most strongly to the later poems in which Graham cultivated a surface of clearness, albeit with the same depths beneath. Their different verbal 'energies', as well as the continuity of their imaginative vision, can be illustrated by tracing the poetic metamorphosis of the sea. In 1946, Graham published 'The Voyages of Alfred Wallis', his tribute to the old fisherman of St Ives whose self-taught paintings of the sea were admired by Ben Nicholson and others. In his Wallis poem, Graham writes of how

> …The holy families of foam
> Fall into wilderness and 'over the jasper sea'.

Graham's diction and imagery evince the early influence of Dylan Thomas: compare Thomas's 'In a cavernous, swung / Wave's silence, wept white angelus knells' for a similarly alliterative sweep of phrase evoking the Christian nativity ('holy families', 'angelus') as a metaphor for the waves' perpetual renewal. The extended description of the sea in Part 3 of 'The Nightfishing' sees Graham beginning to separate the layering of the real and the metaphorical in his language. As the herring boat reaches its fishing ground, throws out its nets and cuts it motor, Graham writes:

> It is us no more moving, only the mere
> Maintaining levels as they mingle together.
> Now round the boat, drifting its drowning curtains
> A grey of light begins. These words take place.

These lines hint at the counterpointed 'levels' of meaning in the whole poem, by which the memory of working on a boat 'mingles' with the present moment of the poet writing. Metaphor mediates between the two voyages: the fishing nets at daybreak become 'drowning curtains', taking us back to the room where 'these words take place'.

Finally, in the poetry that follows 'The Nightfishing', the making of poetry itself becomes the dominant metaphorical act (Greek: metapherein, 'to carry over'), moving between the world as known and the world as imagined. 'The Thermal Stair', Graham's poem for Peter Lanyon, who painted the sea many times, begins:

> I called today, Peter, and you were away.
> I look out over Botallack and over Ding
> Dong and Levant and over the jasper sea.

The verbal music of the previous work is now notably subdued: a chance internal rhyme in the first line, the sing-song anaphora of 'over… over… over…', and the strong, surprising enjambment (perhaps the most distinctive technical device of Graham's later work). Complex orchestration has instead been replaced by a directness of address that is disarmingly close to recorded speech: Graham's friend, Michael Seward Snow, caught the effect nicely when he called it 'an engaging courtesy' that holds us 'painlessly by the ear'.

Everything in these lines can also be read as a statement of fact: Lanyon was a neighbour of Graham's in south-west Cornwall; Botallack, Ding Dong and Levant are the names of tin mines which lie between the higher ground of Madron and the Atlantic; and the colour of that western sea at sunset may well be jasper. But there are also the more ritualistic implications: the poet 'call[s]' to signal the beginning of an elegy, a solemn poem that calls to the dead; there is the onomatopoeic connotation of a slowly tolling funeral bell in 'Ding / Dong' (which will return in the poem's final lines on the 'closing bells' of the Cornish pubs); and 'over the jasper sea' repeats the allusion from Graham's poem about Alfred Wallis to the hymn 'Safe in the Arms of Jesus' by Fanny Crosby ('Over the fields of glory, / Over the jasper sea') – only now without quotation marks to distinguish the language of poetry from the language of daily life.

Graham's friend, the poet and critic Robin Skelton, once wrote that 'every person who has attended a church and sung hymns with a proper sense of their importance has assented to a magical act'. The magical thinking of modern life is not confined to the church in Graham's writing: his poem on the fruit machine in his local pub in Madron, 'Press Button to Hold Desired Symbol', wittily transposes the higher meaning that a reader might hope to 'get' from a poem onto a more mundane form of entertainment. It is the miraculous bareness of Graham's later magic – Prospero drowning his books along the Cornish shore – that continues to charm our century. All metaphysical ideas in his poems are openly presented as make-believe, yet the hopeful emotion that makes belief is not at all diminished by this knowledge: 'Am / I greedy to make you up / Again out of memory?', he asks in another elegy: 'Are you there at all? / I would like to think / You are alright' ('Dear Bryan Wynter').

In an author's note on *Malcolm Mooney's Land*, Graham remarked:

I am always very aware that my poem is not a telephone call. The poet only speaks one way. He hears nothing back. His words as he utters them are not conditioned by a real ear replying from the other side.

The opposition of the poem to the telephone call is strikingly reminiscent of the riddling claim made in 'Personism: A Manifesto' (1959) by the American poet Frank O'Hara:

I was in love with someone […] I went back to work and wrote a poem for this person. While I was writing it I was realizing that if I wanted to I could use the telephone instead of writing the poem, and so Personism was born.

Both Graham and O'Hara now seem highly prescient in their understanding that although lyric poems might adopt a conversational tone, they are not a branch of communications technology. Modern lyric is a lonelier performance of the self in language, which dwells on the difficulty of universal meaning –

a letter in a bottle, as Graham's German contemporary, Paul Celan, saw it, 'en route' to an unknown recipient.

'What is the language using us for?' asks the opening poem of *Implements in Their Places*: 'Have the words ever / Made anything of you'. Such unanswerable questions are echoed by the poets of this anthology, who respond in their own way to Graham's words, voice, humour, drama, landscape, world, myth, magic – all the things he might have meant when he insisted that the most important test of an artist was 'timbre': a distinctively resonant voice. As his friend David Wright wrote in a sixtieth birthday tribute: 'Here is the air I took from you / And here the words I stole'. As an 'entertainment' of many voices, this gathering continues the spirit of wide address, across time and space, in which Graham conceived his own work. Commenting on *Implements*, he mused:

> Maybe this book is going to be more entertaining to more people. Is that what I want? After speaking to myself I suppose I want to speak to the best, whoever they are, alive or dead.

Jeremy Noel-Tod

References

I am indebted to David Whittaker's *Give Me Your Painting Hand: W.S. Graham and Cornwall* (Wavestone Press, 2015), which was a valuable source of biographical detail in writing this introduction. The extracts from Graham's 1949 notebook were published in *Edinburgh Review*, 75 (1987). 'Notes on a Poetry of Release' appeared in *Poetry Scotland*, 3 (1946), and was reprinted as an appendix to *The Nightfisherman: Selected Letters of W.S. Graham* (Carcanet, 2000), ed. Michael and Margaret Snow. Graham's defence of his early poetry is made in a letter to Gavin Saunders, dated 14th April 1981. Michael Seward Snow's remark about Graham's 'engaging courtesy' is quoted on the back cover of *Approaches to How They Behave* (Donut Press, 2009). Robin Skelton's remark on magic is from the chapter on 'Poetry, Magic and Childhood' in his book on poetry for the Teach Yourself series (Hodder and Stoughton, 1963). Paul Celan describes the lyric poem as a letter in a bottle in his 'Speech on the Occasion of Receiving the Literature Prize of the Free Hanseatic City of Bremen' (1958) – see *Collected Prose*, trans. Rosmarie Waldrop (Carcanet, 1986). David Wright's poem 'To W.S. Graham, on his 60th Birthday' first appeared in *The Listener*, 25th January 1979 and was reprinted in his *Metrical Observations* (Carcanet, 1980). Graham's comments on *Malcolm Mooney's Land* and *Implements in Their Places* appeared in the *Poetry Book Society Bulletin* for Spring 1970 and Autumn 1977 respectively. All quotations from Graham's previously published poems are taken from *New Collected Poems*, ed. Matthew Francis (Faber and Faber, 2004).

Editors' Note

The genesis of this anthology can be traced to the discovery at the W.S. Graham estate archive, in spring 2014, of a manuscript copy of Graham's then unpublished poem 'An Entertainment for W.S. Graham for Him Having Reached Sixty-five'. The poem's title brings to mind the late author's 'entertainment' for his friend and fellow poet David Wright, written in June 1979 to mark Wright's approaching sixtieth birthday. Though undated, Graham's poem to himself was possibly composed during the 'spanking summer' of 1983, a few months prior to his sixty-fifth birthday on 19th November of that year. While both poems employ a light, comic tone, there's a striking difference between them. In the former, Graham is quick to write off the importance of any milestone of age, but the fact that he soon felt the need to acknowledge one of his own is not without significance.

By 1983, Graham's health was failing. Years of heavy drinking and poor diet had taken a toll. The symptoms of his final, though as then undiagnosed, illness were causing him difficulty and concern. The poem he drafted during that hot summer is set in Epidaurus, Greece, the healing centre of the Classical world. Despite the metonymic unease brought to bear by the choice of that location, Graham cheekily suggests the work is 'not an auto-elegy'. His characteristic disavowal only heightens the pathos of the poem – a poem in which, perhaps for the first time, his frailty is allowed to be seen.

As Graham's centenary year drew gradually nearer, and archival research began to uncover further striking, unpublished poems, we were aware of Graham's ambivalence toward tribute publication, but the idea of arranging a suitable 'entertainment' for him had taken root. Often in our minds was the unusually wide-ranging admiration of the author amongst poets, with a number of those admirers working from disparate positions within practice. We felt that many would welcome the opportunity of writing in response to Graham's work, especially if they were aware that he might (in a literary sense) attend the party. So, in the spirit of one of W.S. Graham's much-admired poems, we have constructed a space within the confines of this anthology so that something celebratory may move across the caught habits of language between contributors and readers.

*

The W.S. Graham poems published in this anthology contain many dazzling images, phrases and lines of syntactic mastery, though it would be wrong to claim they are amongst his finest work. We do believe, however, they will be of great interest to those acquainted with his poetry. For readers unfamiliar with his writing, we hope this selection will point you to the material Graham chose to publish during his lifetime, which can be found in *New Collected Poems* (Faber and Faber, 2004).

When considering poems abandoned or not definitively completed by the author, we decided that all candidate poems should exist in at least one completed draft and be of notable artistic interest. An exception to the former caveat was made; the poem '[Late Between Disguises]' is a tantalising fragment. The selection of 'implements' included were drawn from a number of archival sources, though the vast majority were recovered from the Robin Skelton Special Collection at the University of Victoria, British Columbia, Canada, by Nathan Hamilton and David Nowell Smith.

Where no title was indicated by W.S. Graham himself, we have followed the practice adopted by Margaret Blackwood and Robin Skelton in *Aimed at Nobody* (Faber and Faber, 1993) and then continued by Matthew Francis in *New Collected Poems*: titles chosen by the editors are enclosed in square brackets. Graham's creative use of spelling and punctuation are well known. We have only corrected typographical errors where we each felt certain of them. House style, likewise, has been sensitively applied in the knowledge that Graham submitted his work to a similar process during his lifetime. Source notes for W.S. Graham poems can be found on pages 258 and 259.

*

During the preparation of this anthology, we became acquainted with a large number of previously published tributes to W.S. Graham – some produced by his friends and contemporaries. Despite our appreciation of these poems, historical publishing biases led us to a decision to include only a relatively small number, thereby leaving a considerable space for work written leading up to the centenary by authors writing from a diverse range of backgrounds and poetic practices.

*

Twelve of the poems contributed to *The Caught Habits of Language* will also appear on the Scottish Poetry Library website during the months of W.S. Graham centenary year, as poems from The Blue Crevasse. The image of a blue crevasse famously appears in Graham's poem 'Malcolm Mooney's Land', and the author's estate welcomed the idea of creating a similar metaphorical space where admirers of the poet might, in a sense, be lowered for a month's solitary 'residency'.

*

Our anthology title derives from Graham's own poetry and highlights key facets of it – the importance of language and community, and the need for humour. Despite its complexities, W.S. Graham's poetry is distinctive in its inclusivity. We have prepared *The Caught Habits of Language* in that spirit.

The Caught Habits of Language

An Entertainment for W.S. Graham
for Him Having Reached One Hundred

These words said welcome. Fare
Them well from what they are

'Letter I', W.S. Graham

Alan Gillis

The Interior

There is a bed.
There is a bedside cabinet,
a clock. There are no adjectives.
Whiteness is painted on two walls,
on two walls there is wallpaper
with boats on waves.
There is a window, a window
sill. There are no curtains
but blinds. There is a desk,
a desk chair. There is nothing on the desk.
There is a wardrobe, whose door
is closed. There is nothing else.

If we draw the blinds, open the window,
let adjectives in, we can see
there is not much bedness about the bed,
sloped and low, no view out the window;
not much you might call beddy-bye
with sheets a bleached who cares non-colour
as if ironed by an enormous
angry iron: you wouldn't dream
of sailing the high seas in there.
The cabinet could bore description to death
and the clock can no longer face
blank nights, the stale air.

The whiteness painted on two walls is off-
white the way a joke can be off
or a person. The window blinds snigger
like blades, cutting the anonymous room
from the anomalous moon-shaped streetlamp
floating on the black sea of night outside.
I ate crab claws on a boat that set out

from Donaghadee towards Fort William
once and it was awful, the sea a grey
soup of seasickness, sky a freezing fog.
The dippy orange Yellow Submarine-style
cartoon boats on the wallpaper are off

on a repeating trip over abstract
wave lines that jag symmetrically
rather than crest, repeating at ten
centimetre intervals. One might guess
that if anything was written on
that desk it might be gibberish but we
shall refrain from prejudicial speculation.
A lifetime of work to own a house
then you end up diminished by it.
A lifetime of work to find a voice
then you end up imprisoned by its
drone when you try to rise

to the occasion. Keener readers
will have noted there is no floor,
no ceiling. I recall standing, feeling
I was sinking, outside a bedroom
window one freezing dawn, the sky a grey
formless soup, having paced the night
to nowhere in particular – to this
window – I suppose thinking if this is home
then I'm at sea, at sea. At intervals
from then to now I have set out to find
walls, a row of rooms, strange worlds
within the wardrobe, whose door is closed.

Tony Williams

Reading WSG at Loch Earn

The half-waves of untidal waters wash
a shore of broken ears and bend their glass
to stretch a 'landscape' into something else.

The jetty's rotten teeth are eating air.
The water quickens with its thousand silvery tongues.
Yours is the voice to mend that rock, the thought

that stitch by stitch should quilt itself to nub
the valley's narrow dish. Your unheld
holdings on and back becrannog it.

Here is moss and here is bracken stamped
by thinking tactful of itself. And here is cold,
cold water draining through the stones

yet lapping on in short insistent phrases
that don't end. Above, against, across
the road the burns like tiny murmurs run

from every shrug of moor to fill a loch
which quakes to pass the rumours on to wash
and bless and make the hearing whole,

a speechless doctoring or teasing lip
to thread me through the needle of this place
and tie me here when I am gone.

Zaffar Kunial

W*nd

When I arrived
I didn't know
the word
for what I was.

I kept arriving.
Butting my head
against the shore.
A head with no word.

And one day
I heard. And it heard
that what I was
was wind. The one

w*nd, I was
the rumour of my own being.
A groundless rumour
in residence.

*

Sure I said. Sure.
Though I wasn't
and have never
been. Shore I said.

Repeating their word
for where I had brought
them. But no shore
was ever a harbour

for me. Never home
entirely. Where are
all four directions
home? Or when?

Sure. I said sure.
Repeating their word
for this coastal state
where I'm never entirely.

*

W, w, w…
Between the wires
weather from elsewhere
becomes ours.

Another aloneness
checks in with us, checks us
where stops meet starts.
Entering like my old stutter.

Perhaps the beginning
was the ultimate abbreviation
or silver cord. Aeolus,
a god with all

vowels but one,
knotted the winds in an ox skin.
All the swirling directions a word
could go, but home. West, west.

*

Wis, wis. In the beginning
w, w, w… It's the *was*
not the *Word* I stutter at, before I
arrive, in *w* and *s*

at the aleph, or alif
that blows me into being.
To the in of the in. The black
of the star, reversed to when all that

was began, before solar w*nd,
intergalactic w*nd,
a first breath from beyond
my bond, my vowel.

A wavering oneness
or wand. One's shyest
earliest wound
unwound.

Helen Tookey

Boat

St Michael's Bay, Cornwall

So did you maybe dream it – that wrecked boat
uncovered by storm, by shifted sand,
for just one day? A year and more

you'd walked that beach in all weathers
and there'd never been a boat: only that day,
the day she left you, and you walked the beach

as always, because what else could you do
– only that day was there a boat, bleached and broken,
a thing of ribs, with just enough hull

to make a holding; so you crept inside, curled up
and lay for hours, until the sheer indifference
of wind and sea brought some kind of peace

and next day again there was no boat
and when you asked you were told
there had never been a boat; and maybe not dream

but surely deep need had fetched it, if only
for those few hours, back into its being
as a thing that holds, that keeps afloat –

Denise Riley

Three Awkward Ears

I

It rains it rains shepherdess, rains on the river – as
if on thicker liquids, cream or latex, raindrops stot it
to pitted rings in water, which swell to hoops of water.

Up gallop young men, each of them pleasingly sharpened
to hunt down dormant crepitus in smooth sprawled limbs
since, speaking botanically, flowering's a sign of distress.

Beribboned looms the large one, stolid in his pale satin
who was ever gravely loving but was not much loved back –
he's ruffed for the arching gleam and flop of tulip heads.

Some buxom clouds lollop along, gloweringly under-lit
past russet trees brushed dark, fine-feathered by sable hair.
What's that inhuman call, far into the woods of no ears.

II

High confident calling

to no one it knows of

from no throaty talker

nor squirreled in ears

it fans out to soar over

gaping-jawed screens

or dilate that one iris as

purplish as hearts whose

it isn't – so, pulsating to

mouth every anyone, it

uncoils as invoking –

opens its confiding peal.

III

ice-burned tongues
clump into celestine's
eye-blue spar & chink
on snow-muffled ears

SOUND a long blast
Of silence CUT

'Wynter and the Grammarsow', W.S. Graham

Tim Cumming

The Sound

The sound returned often,
a companion for much
of our journey that day.
It tended to travel ahead of us,
accompanied by a range of subtle
chemical changes in the atmosphere
upon which the first religions
had been laid. We heard it
on the wind, then in the heart,
where it seemed to divide
into separate sources,
and the light in it was marvellous.
Great care and a range of nutritional
restrictions were indicated,
and kept us there in silence for many hours.
Under magnification, what seemed
to be entanglement from a distance
appeared to retreat the closer we
appeared to come to revealing ourselves,
until it was just the two of us at
the end of the day in a small room
that held a wilderness, the still
point of the returning world, its sound
in the distance pushing us forward
until we had located its source.

Alan Buckley

Confessional

'I knew these people'
Travis Henderson, *Paris, Texas*

Maybe this is like that booth –
I'm Harry Dean Stanton and
you're Nastassja Kinski. You
can't see me, and my back's turned
towards you, as I husk out
these words into the white phone.
You hear my disembodied
voice through the little speaker.
Love. Obsession. Alcohol.
Jealousy. You smooth your hair:
your grey eyes flicker and fill
with tears as you realise
this story's not just about
me. This is your story too.

Or maybe I'm Nastassja.
Although you think you can see
me, make-up's part of my trade.
I'm only ever who you
want me to be. Even when
I press my hands to the glass
and you turn, it's your ghost's face
that's staring back at you, framed
by my blonde bob. I won't stop
turning my tricks. Look around
at all that whiteness: in three
lines you'll drive off into it,
believing we really met,
that somehow you've been redeemed.

Dai George

The Continual Other Offer

'So I would have it, waved from home to out
After that, the continual other offer…'
                    'The Nightfishing', W.S. Graham

Wind on a dry night, raking
the last barely scented lees of spring
into the room whose window I must pry apart
to sleep less wildly at your side.

Over and beyond us grinds the enterprise
I covet: the racked and breathless sea
hauling its discoveries from shelf to shelf
and down into the ever-lost museum
where I struggle through unquiet hours
to swim. It is here I could do anything,

where the drowning beckons me, and air is
day shining squarely on a wave yet farther out.
I reach for you deeper down, in the dormitory
dark, still panicking and wet. Anything means
anything: the flush of my hand against you turned
to murder, a lapse in self, unthinkable except

I thought it – and who here would reproach me
but the wind? That wind is devilish, my love.
It champs in the pane, a proposal overheard
from a shoreline that I swore I'd never breach.

Emily Critchley

In Memory W.S. Graham

It's late. Call off the knives of language subtly
drawn, funereal. Take significance
with you. Each chosen moment, each

abject tender thing, wound tight
& hurt across the dark, that whitens naked
with dawn. Don't drive into that

rhyme knowing what you know:
how it will all end. The story's not
yet straight with me & lyric I

's become unfashionable again. Or we
have borne too much not to go on.
Each singing choice, each incisive error

could have been different & we know it,
we, who wanted that alive or dead,
but to be real. Or we have come too

far not to give in. And feelings
aren't that way inclined, aren't natural
phenomena. Yes but they are.

Now not one edge left to bleed you with?
Probably it doesn't matter.
Probably the heart's a free-flowing

instrument, stupid place, directionless.
And now that's hardly occurred,
now you, the text, can all agree on nothing.

Vona Groarke

The Choosing

'Under the poem's branches two people
Walk and even the words are shy.'
      'The Secret Name', W.S. Graham

Well then, let morning be a pair of yellow boots
drilling into the edge of the wood.
Or have it be the wood with the yellow boots
lining everything up to their stride.
Either way, we get where we're going
or else, lost, footless, doubling back,
we decide those two words on that tree stump
were left there for us two to find.

So take it from me this morning, do,
two secondhand, blue-veined possible roads –
one for the forest, one for the shore.
Between them, the choosing. And us.

Through the forest on one side is visible
a field lit by sunflowers or rape;
the other side has its back to the field
and shoulders a darkness with two sounds in it –
a yellowhammer and a woodpecker
that hammers out, insistently,
the news that everything will be wonderful
or else that everything won't.
That either the trees will shelter you
as you huddle with your dry words
or they'll crowd your head
so no light gets through

until your fingers separate the branches,
flip back the clumped hammers
on your Underwood
or lately hit RTN on Word
so the screen yawns wide
as a clearing, dry hole,
that my day falls hard into, like rain.

Do not disturb me now. I have to extract
A creature with its eggs between the words

'Language Ah Now You Have Me', W.S. Graham

Mel Pryor

In a Secondhand Bookshop

Here's his signature, W S Graham,
in tidy pencil inside a first edition
of *Alanna Autumnal* by George Barker.
And he's written the date, August
1944. And the place, Cornwall.
Back then he was twenty-five, at war
with the war, living in a caravan
near Sydney Cove. Picture him there,
sprawled on a cramped bench bed,
feet up against the caravan window
as he pulls this book back on its hinges
and reads, lifting his eyes only occasionally
to the scraps of cloud above Pengersick Lane,
until the clouds become stars,
until he moves into that next world,
beyond Cornwall and beyond books,
of dreams. Did it have, the caravan,
man-made light? Don't tell me
it wasn't the sun and then the moon
that lit his way from word to word
down Barker's trail of young sentences.
Maybe I buy the book in the brief belief
that thoughts can be reciprocal
and travel back and forth through time.
Maybe I want to feel his hand under
my own hand as I turn the old pages and read
*We have nothing left for us to do but sicken
at the magnificence of our predecessors.*

Katharine Towers

The Good Words

The world as it is we can see for ourselves –
yellow corn, brick wall, bird-
table, reading book, the odd bad apple.
Most beautiful are the beginning words
(carbon, darkness, bad apple).
We use the world to put our language
into use, parsing back to clinch the thing
that's in the wrappings of the symbol.

Take from a river any thought of endlessness
or death to find it's only water on its way.
Neither is the tired old moon a mother
or a maiden or a crone.

Imagine a real garden where I sit
with my soul in dead November leaves,
thinking of your good words like fox,
and bower and bramble.

Lavinia Singer

A Voice Between Two Things

world   spaces
       imagined   gestures
through   empty
       significant   shapes
the sea   as
       the sea   spinning
visual   disturbances
       my   other
side of   language
       invisible   to you
the construct   a silence
       calligraphic   dream
drawing   thing
       made   abstract
sky-trekking   new
       uncommon   words
time or   oneself
       or   how alone
one is   released
       into the   human

Fiona Benson

Song for the Rabbit Man

The butcher's back, tying his knots
in the hedge. His red-eyed ferret
pours itself down rabbit holes,
flushing out the burrows,

their many exits mined and countermined –
a warren's an exploded wound –
tick-tock, tick-tock, the ferret seeks,
all the slip-routes noosed, besieged,

the whole ridge seined
by the butcher's clever hands.
Through naked thorn I catch
the long, balletic arc

of the oatmeal-coloured buck
the butcher holds at his waist.
Back at his shop he eases the corpse
out of its coat like a lover,

tender to all the weeping cisterns of the body,
the slick little heart,
the bladder's pissy sac,
the sphincter's slender wedding band.

Dusk at the hedge and the doe
noses out of her nest.
Her horseshoe womb is a sharp new moon,
seven kits are ripening in their seven rooms.

The buck's lean meat
with its dark placental taste of roots
is iron on the tongue,
a quick thing gone, beginning.

Hugh MacDiarmid

The Royal Stag

The hornless heart carries off the harem,
Magnificent antlers are nothing in love.
Great times are only a drawback and danger
To the noble stag that must bear them.

Crowned as with an oaktree he goes,
A sacrifice for the ruck of his race,
Knowing full well that his towering points
Single him out, a mark for his foes.

Yet no polled head's triumphs since the world began
In love and war have made a high heart thrill
Like the sight of a Royal with its Rights and Crockets,
Its Pearls, and Beam, and Span.

Because always language
Is where the people are

'The Dark Dialogues', W.S. Graham

Marion McCready

Night Crossing

The ferry hums through unseen waves;
strip lighting flickering above our heads,
late night conversations struggle around us.
The streetlights of Gourock grow smaller.
Squinting, I transform the orange balls
into rows of glowing crosses,
calvaries, ascending the black hillside.

I've been here before, many times –
my sixteenth birthday
when he proposed on the upper deck
in the heart of this dark estuary
against the backdrop of Orion
and the Seven Sisters.
The land-lights are drifting further
away as we sail deeper into the Firth;
life swarming beneath us –
basking sharks, mackerels, silver eels,
a colony of flame shells, sewing themselves
together on the seabed.

We skim across the surface of the Clyde,
across dark waves and into dark skies.
I imagine my mother's final crossing
strapped to the ambulance bed, breathing
through an oxygen mask, like a struggling
high altitude climber or deep-sea diver.
The streetlights form signals now,
signs from dry land, the intermittent blip
of car lights, journeying the shore line –
a sort of Morse code, message
from the other side.

Sasha Dugdale

Headland

Waxy sporadic grass knitting the sand…

A loudspeaker on a car proceeds slowly up the far quay
and a wedge of sandpipers lifts in fright from the shore:
The circus king is back for one last stand!
Last performance of the season – tonight!

His old gardening jacket hangs like a phantom behind the door
I have a febrile energy for undoing endings
tying the old twine to new twine, so when he came to me in a dream
and asked to come back I was surprised
to find myself rejecting him one last time

pouring myself a solitary drink of seawater
and reminding him of how we saw the old vessel of his body
and it was no longer fit-for-purpose
could not be recycled or rewound
like string, or green glass or driftwood.

The whole place reeks of him, who in life smelt of railways
sugar soap and the commuter tang. Sand, salt,
thrift and rotting wrack, and stubbornness:
a vast firewood stack, a few elderly tools revived
with rags and oily fingers to massage working parts,

string tied into rolls of barbed wire.
I am walking today on the hollow old dune
September chill, the children are off buying shoals
of pencils and the circus cut-outs on the sand bank
are blanketed up for the year.

What are years? They last no longer than the tide.
I read the tables, I pore over them and seem to find relief
in the mathematical appearance of water
and how by degrees it creeps upon us,
another ten metres to swill around the back gate.

Last performance of nostalgia out here, where it burns
with an acrid smell. Throw on an armful of regret, it fires up
odd-flamed like rubber or plastic flotsam
or household chemicals glugging themselves empty.
My fingers smell like his.

seaskin~early-white-haired
furious~sea-martyrdom~worth
seawork~surrounding~searopes
beside~emerald~seadeep~sea-show
sea-marching~to~sealaw~into
seaside's~seabent~seawalls

seadogged~scaled~reined
bubbled~filled~wrecked
skidding~seafared~on
whispered~
well~
only~

fingerprints, in dreams, become
warmth in warmth, identified
and not identifiers.
who laps the swing of a sky
where triumph and vertigo
don't lock down on darker eyes?

put up and shut up, the gold
of a horse of dreams canters
the inheld field of my blood.
in your museums, I found
me, lady, right at your side.

seastrolling~find~seadoors
into~seashelled~pulses
sealogged~seachanged~through
calling~seaware~seavessels
lie~break~seanight's
endured~seavessel~moves

seaport

Vahni Capildeo

Seastairway

ofer wæpema gebind
'The Wanderer'

We sail

a~a~a~the~the~the~the
sea-troughs~sea-tombs~seawalls
the~the~the~the~this~that~my
seafarer~seawalker~seasaint
her~their~sea-lamb~seafriend
wandered~outlined~holy~crowded

wait for it: waiting occurs
in waves *put up and shut up*
the hand is undomestic
at this scale: ice-dipped, might be
a beak, cormorant, gannet;
might be a scientific
instrument, ice-proof; is in
a bind. you know, if you know,
you'll *put up and shut up*. sleep
only, sleep alone, brings hands
out of the scale of exile;

with~seabelled~seanight
in~seaful~seawind
searoped~sea-tongued~seagreat
over~seabord~seaside
down~seamist~seagrain
seacircling~seabraes~sea-gentled

Kathryn Gray

Difficult Ones

Thirteen years, my difficult ones!
And what have I become?

This morning I set myself down
in the small room again,

its aspect on rain and time
being nothing if not instructive.

I contemplate water and glass.
What are you saying? I practise

in the ham tones of a lovers' silence,
which is all the same not loneliness –

not quite – my difficult ones,
since at the least absence

is a form of the lightness beginning.
Beautiful mutes,

how you crowd at the pane
of the mind – in each bead your faces

wild, your mouths the shape of
Not I! Not I!

Or so I am willed to imagine.
It is always April

on the tongue. Nothing is
begun again, yet something

cleaves or cleaves to sense.
My art is in the limerence.

David Wheatley

Roger Hilton, November '64

'We either touch or do not touch'
across the tides that circulate
from Cornish sound to silver north;
in nets of colour, past the Firth,
we find our misplaced eyes too late
in deeper-than-deep blues you catch.

A spar, a prow, a rock, the sun:
they are not fixed but follow courses
framing patterns known to brush
and nib alone, now smooth, now harsh;
take our tributes with our curses
who helpless face the storm-waves down.

A man is gathering limpets from
the shore past which the trawlers scud
like fairground nags that rise and fall,
gauzed in the haar through which I feel
our ruin drawn tight like a coat
with not one light to see us home.

Sydney Graham reach me a hand.
I read behind the forms a tale
that falls away and leaves the forms,
the floods of light that burst their frames
and bursting launch the canvas sail
I still believe can find your strand.

Bear these words in mind
As they bear me soundly
Beyond my reach

'Letter VII', W.S. Graham

W.S. Graham

[*To Sheila Lanyon On the Flyleaf of a Book*]

Sheila, we speak here on the fly
Leaf of a book which was myself
    A good few graves ago.
Now I am maintained by other
Words for better or for worse
    To whisper my hello.

The seasons turn. Threshold on thresh
Hold forms continually and falls
    Under grief's lonely hammer.
What did you say? I thought between
These fly leaf words I heard you speak
    Out of your Second Summer.

The summer chimes and turns its blue
Dragon-flying eyes to see
    We two are not afraid.
Hello, Sheila, I can hear
Your breath on the other side of the word
    And see you turn your head.

W.S. Graham

Evening on Loch Long

For a change I look at you
Here held burnished only
By your eye and the gull's
Long Gaelic cry.
I am your memory teased
Out into a wisp
And glint of the going
Light into the west.

I knew you well, young,
Inspecting the oystercatching
Long sea-wrack ledges.
Then, later, you took
That half-cousin of yours
Rowing on (As you say.)
My highland bosom. O
Don't rush off yet for you
Have rushed away far
Too much down your own
Long loch of memory.

My hills, my bracken sides,
My banks are in the shade
Now and you may go
But still with the young end
Of your tether held
Always still here.

W.S. Graham

[*The Boundaries*]

The West Boundary. It salts your face
And the great bird Mull of Oa
Is not for you. Your big half-crown
To Rory stirring the mash will not
Entitle you to anything but
A visitor's careful Gaelic. Where
In what silence are you residing now?

The East Boundary. I'll rub the hollow
Between your shivering blades
From the North Sea of the herring banks.
By hearth of Moeder, or sewing snapped
Meshes on pebbles on the blind har,
On this side you will be confined.
This silence allows you to say its shape.

The South Boundary. Might be your undoing.
I can't see where you are in the geo
Graph of the silence I have put you in.
Anyhow this is where you stop
Southward. The Latinatudinous tombs
Of language will open and put you deep
Onto the southern third edge.

The North Boundary. It is not
In your nature to go up there
To make your life more likable
To where you lurk. I saw you freezing
Numbing between the cakes of ice.
That will stop you there saying
Anything. I saved your life.

W.S. Graham

[*Less Than the Edge of a Rain Flute*]

1

Less than the edge of a rain flute
Dipping into the morning Gitings
Finds the girl and boy.

Also there is a linnet
Observing flying asking
For information and saying see
You two see who I am.

The couple are not watching
Or even themselves or each other
Cast away on the Gitings.

2

The light with high intelligence
Looks over Cleeve Hill
Down at the racecourse fences.

    Palings posts railings white
    Guarders of the different beasts.

And is so fine the girl's lashes
Soak in darkness.

    I'll meet thee on the Gitings
    On the steep summer side.

3

Or if you like stay.
Be some beast glistening
With rain in a poem lying high
Above and out of sight of
Your children the little gallopers.

                    Less than the edge
                    Of a rain flute
                    Keeps us cast
                    Away here
                    On the top of the Gitings.

W.S. Graham

[*Late Between Disguises*]

Make up your mind. Come in. You're lucky
To catch me here so late between
Disguises. I can see by your face
You are a mister of some importance

Or are you a Northern Earl? I said this
And he sat down and brushed the hail
Off his shoulders. We said nothing.
(Excuse me. May I look at what
I have put down. I want to make it
Right for you and your children running
Into the English language.) Anyhow,
This creature enters with epaulettes
Of hail and here we sit with no
Interpreter to change English
Into English. Too loud outside
To hear the Madron owl. I think
I see him going to speak. My cat
Not looking sees him almost beginning
To say something. What shall we do?

W.S. Graham

Or from Your Emerald Office are You Able

Hide your looking face
Blackened by the ice
Behind the words. Did I forget to tell
Malcolm you were a great reader but fragile?
Or from your emerald office are you able
To return with messages
From the glass ages?

My dear my furry reader,
Please knock at the door
And stand there icicled and burnt with frost.
Sometimes within the words we can get lost
And not know what to do. I think the last
Whipend of the journey
Still wants to carry
Us off in the long black
Sledge to find us something.

Hold tight hold tight and into the abstract night
We go with no right to expect anything.

W.S. Graham

For Robert Brennan

Dear Robert, replying with words to stone
Tonight, I heft your solid scored
Fashioned slate in my writing hand.
Gravity loves it and the ground
It was wrenched from would understand.

It speaks you very well with scrived
Unparallels and that one black
Concavity that watches me.
Speak, fucking slatey chunk, to me
Who weighs you with humility.

I hold it and my animal hand
Darkens the oblongs as they drink
My oils in. I draw slowly
My nail across the runes I see.
And the hidden rune speaks secretly.

W.S. Graham

[*What We Call the World*]

Is what we call the world
Punishing you more
Than me? I mean is your
Threshold higher and if
So how do you know? I knew
A man who wept at blue.

A man who wept at green.
I cannot bear to be tortured.
I mean I cannot bear
To change my torture. Age
Is easing me away.
It is as though the sea

I had a relationship with
And employed so casually
Is rushing in with new
Prongs and cruel capsizes
To seek my tender places.

W.S. Graham

The Contemporary Dear

Come then, the Chisel Temperer
    And come the Water Man.
Come all you that encounter
    The black or white or tan.
Come all you that encounter
    The word that's like a stone.
My own contemporary dear
    I am yours alone.

These are only words now
    That blow up from my kin,
And here now at my lamp
    They let the winged ghosts in.
Come in like Goya ghosts
    Winging from the moon.
My own contemporary dear
    I am yours alone.

I have wedged the sashes
    Against the knocking dead
And trimmed my lamp against
    The might of Gurnard's Head.
O here at this table
    I have sat so long.
My own contemporary dear
    I am yours alone.

Now it is the late light
    Knuckle at the door,
The visitor who visits
    The word from afar.
The knuckle is bent back
    To a tight white bone.
My own contemporary dear
    I am yours alone.

Never to hear it better
    The master in his place
Waits for silence
    To turn round its face.
Come you mothy faces
    That thud the windowpane.
My own contemporary dear
    I am yours alone.

No two can meet the way that we have met,
Completely, like the marriage of fused stars

'To ND', W.S. Graham

Ian Duhig

Glass Words

1 Deep Ballad Very Not

My glass, half-full, toasts absent friends
    and absences per se,
the room for rhyme this mummer begs
    and the nothing that he says.

Graham's mother brought Irish ballads
    over her white threshold
lamenting boys in a border war
    that like them won't grow old.

They crossed the borders of his poems
    and got behind his lines
as foggy dew or Kevin's song
    or some free-floating sign.

But Graham's line breaks spell out more
    than rafts of black on white;
his starboard margins docked his craft,
    its sail the page he wrote

with all his windows flags of ink
    and Nessie sleeping sound,
for deeper than the deep he loved
    his Nessie and his friends.

The sea O the sea, the geal grá
    mo chroí, long may she flow
between silence and poetry,
    where his words come and go.

I press my ear to his black pane
    to catch his breath and language
these words and glass are raised to now.
    His own would burn this page.

2 Pangur Dubh, Pangur Bán

... *In that deep ballad very not*
A dream. Driving to the Borders,
I heard Geordies rhyme Graham
with dream. In mine, I wake him,

a man of many parts and a part
of many men, disjecta membra,
a Franklinstein crossing his floe,
his old element frozen to a blank

sheet waiting for prints, the head
of a glass of Mooney's Irish Stout,
a communion moon a lost mouse
might cross and keep its paws dry.

Irish monks invented the pause
of space between words in texts
where Graham wrote his home
between this word and the next.

One monk wrote a margin poem
about his white cat Pangur Bán
hunting mice as he for meanings,
all escaping through translation,

Flower's flowery and Auden's flat.
Graham's marginal poem 'Pangur'
has the hunted poet lament his fate,
being caught in a ridiculous dream.

Now he's in this ridiculous poem,
or his reiver name is at least: but if
you're dry or not, drink to Graham
who caught and shared all. Not half.

Nessie Dunsmuir

For a Winter Lover

I should have been more scrupulous
of that first hour.
More measured against future loss
the live and lovely hazard where
soul signalled soul
through body's tenderness.
But what had loss to do with us
held there and holding all
the blinding universe?

Stranger in my arms
man clown and angel
bearing like flowers
the everlasting annunciation.

I do not know and never shall
what grave or joyful mystery
inhabits your head's holiness,
but my strong heart has made your ease,
my eyes inherit a lightstruck world.

Sarah Howe

Waking

These heavying months, my nights have bobbed in your wake –
quiet passenger in your heart-lulled craft, asleep
to the glaring world of after. Soon we will make

our introductions: this is called a *home*, this *tree*,
that bite at your cheek is *winter*. You can't yet hear
our voices' muffled cello; your dial's tuned to sea.

My steps lengthen and slow, but my fears lope before
me: laid out on a gurney (gut a sinking stone)
I'll strain to hear the ocean pitching at your door

and find the room silent. Unthink it. I will take
each day by waiting day until we hear your cry
rise among the liquid stars gathering as you wake.

Charles Causley

Letter to W.S. Graham

Dear Sydney, or
Should I call
You Willie,
I don't know

Which. We only
Met once and
Didn't call each
Other anything.

Sitting here in
The thick bit
Of Cornwall
Watching the day

Move round my
Two cypress trees
I was thinking of
You and Nessie down

At the sharp end,
Enduring as usual
The first bite of
The Atlantic. I

Heard you were
Ill and hope
You're bettering.
One thing, your

Poetry was never
Under that sort
Of weather. I
Turn to it as to

A spring that has
Not failed me in
Forty years. In
Your fishbone

Tweed, silk
Stock and glass
Shoes you looked
To me like a

1st War Colonel
(Ret.) and not
The Wild Man
Of Madron I'd

Been warned to
Expect. But like
All poets, you were
In disguise; a

Good one, too;
Though when you
Said a few
Words on my

Behalf from the
Dead body
Of the Hall at
That reading I

Feared you might
Say something
Awful. Like. Or.
But it was O.

K. I thank you;
Think of you as
The Genuine Miracle
Working Icon

Man wandering
Starved and wind-
Scraped Zennor
Where the cows

If not the
Poets ate the
Bell-ropes.
The day I

Called with the
Fan from Germany
There was no reply
To doortaps and

You weren't in
The pub either.
Maybe you were
There all the

Time and took no
Notice. If so,
Fine. Noticing should
Be put to better

Uses. So continue
Listening for
The sound the land
Makes, the signals

The ocean sends, the
Secret speeches of
Air and fire as
You move about the

Scrubbed bracken,
The simple strong
Flowers, the written
And unwritten stones,

In the long fret of
The sea. You will always
Be there for me, always
Standing at the gate

Of Madron Black
Wood, a salt
Poem in your ever
Greenock hand.

Peter Riley

A *Prelude for W.S.G.*

'Very gently struck
The quay night bell.

Now…'

An ordinary and barely noticeable event
written into a free harmony, just as it was.
Hark! now I hear it, ding, just once.
                    You see, Mr Graham,
I was gently struck when my father died,
'moving out past the islands' taking all his
unfinished business with him. I hear him now
saying, 'I'm sorry. I shouldn't have died,
it upsets people, and there is enough
death in the world as it is.' I'm sorry, I say
(and the bell moves slightly in the quay wind
without, I think, sounding) I didn't treat you better.
I was not free, I didn't know you on the open page
where all bells ring and songs sing themselves
over the sea, the gobbling sea waiting for us all.
I was still in my imaginary harbour. I remember
your departing incomprehension and help-
lessness that hangs in my speech now like
a bell barely rung. Language is never enough.
The bell so close to ringing, a tear, perhaps,
an imaginary tear, falls on it from the real world,
the night of thought where when it rings it is heard.
And hearing it, we know. Well,
                    I'll leave you now, Mr Sydney,

to your alcohol evening, coming home late
on the cliff path with the last star burning
by your foot, and in through your own front door.
And just then, when a closure is pending,
the quay night bell very gently tolls
and we know, we are all called out.

A.B. Jackson

Supper with the Grahams

It's flour-and-water
pancake night

Gurnard's Head
our chef Sydney

paraffin fuel
Nansen primus

Nessie rockbound
scavenging limpets

the cat even
is fussy with them

Are you hungry Sydney
Aye undernourished

No butters no simple
sugars no pemmican

Consider Franklin
who snacked on shoes

who masticated
reindeer moss

his crew at meat
cold buttocks brains

a litter of shins
nibbled clean

Traversing the white
waste who wins

where's dwelling now
some ice-burrow

language spoils
journals blackened

soot from Sydney's
midnight stove

II Nessie

Nothing not me was floated on the first waters.
Your image came to settle on my eyes.

The slounging sunlight of your sea-flung word:
what recompense in what strange coinage.

I would have chosen children, breathing hearth,
not this wordy ferment in the fingers.

Borrow me back from Easter's cross and kiss:
I am that acorn, mile, miracle, tree.

Here by the window, elder and blackthorn
sail their bright dayshift down.

The Easter fields of children turn again
in darkness dropping its silent name.

Language is expensive if
We want to strut, busked out
Showing our best on silence

'Approaches to How They Behave', W.S. Graham

Matthew Sweeney

Sausages

There are six of you, inhabiting the same gut,
twisted separate. You lie on the white plate,
coiled, like fat, sleeping worms, waiting

waiting on the hot pan with spitting oil
after the knife frees you. In each of you
is my long-dead grandfather, and the pigs

the pigs he killed, then cleavered in the yard,
their last squeals too, then the hard journey,
twice, through the mincer to the big bowl

the big bowl where chopped onion joins them,
also wild thyme, garlic, breadcrumbs, parsley,
salt, and a good dash of pepper. The pig gut

the pig gut is removed and cleaned in water,
so the mixture can be squeezed in, the gut
twisted at intervals, and you are ready

ready, so my grandfather lights a cigarette,
opens a bottle of Guinness and swigs it,
sitting down at the far end of the table

the table I will sit at when you're browned,
and I'll eat you, one by one, with mustard,
raising a black glass to my grandfather.

Niall Campbell

Cooling a Meal by the Outside Door

Two minutes to set things in order:
this pale heat lifting from the bowl
and the slight, noticeable lift
of moisture from the rain-soaked ground

balanced with the sun falling and
the leaf-fall from the guttering.
Devotee of, what, if not small actions,
I stir heat – and, my own good life
running away with me, I pair
things up: tree with moon, streaming clouds

with this child's bowl – small works of love
and this dim porch. The night sky opens
and, here, the meal is cool; the meal
is cool and, here, the night sky opens.

Peter Gizzi

A Round for W.S. Graham

Surely there are words
lost and gone astray
Tuned and re-
maining a name
Hyacinth, poppy, rose
Sun above, sky below
What of the day's
open distance
Enter yourself and
enter a mouth
The small nouns
build this surround
Call them back and
place them here
Repurposed and alive
Surely there are words
lost and gone awry
And then what of
the thing itself
A field and
a tree and a hill
Enter a noun
and open the day
Surely there are words
lost and gone astray
Call them back and
place them here
Hyacinth, poppy, rose
Sun above, sky below
Repurposed and tuned
Tuned and re-
maining a name
Surely there are words

lost and gone awry
And then what of
the thing itself
What of the day's
open distance
A field and
a tree and a hill
The small nouns
build this surround
Enter yourself and
enter a mouth
Enter a noun
and open the day

Carrie Etter

One for London

after W.S. Graham

Language, let's traipse.
I am in milk-grey London
with white wine and a fine mood.
Though I put my back to it,

the jazz is coming for me.
Language, I'm going to need you
shortly, if I'm going to sustain
the moment's teeming.

The saxophone slithers behind
the double bass. Why name the night
when I'm in London and
wildebeest and language and wine?

Matthew Welton

Which of us is it I am?

How long could we live off peanuts and pickles?
What about whisky? Whose photograph's that?
What's the word for what it means to feel no
doubt you feel no doubt? Will you sell me your
pencil? How deep is the mist?

How would I know if you were taping our
conversations? What's in the water? Who was in
the hammock? Is the radio okay or is it just the
signal? Why buy a ticket if you're not taking the
train?

What about the wasps? Did you wind your watch
this morning? Is anybody going to finish this
soup? What will we do if, with no movement
from us, the shadows of our hands make gestures
of their own?

What's in the jam jar? Whose sneakers are those?
Didn't you send the postcards until you'd come
home? Shouldn't we leave a note to say which
road we'll be taking? Is the tape still running? Is
this bridge on the map?

What if the breadth of our definitions doesn't
depend on our definition of breadth? Who wants
a lemon? How easily do you bruise? What is
there to stop me rejigging your words to make
them say something you might not mean?

How old's your toothbrush? Where'd you put the paracetamol? Won't you be feeding the fishes? Does meaning make up for the absence of melody? When is a reason not a reason? Isn't there more chocolate?

Where did you learn to punch that hard? Where did you leave the suitcase? Could you sell me a stamp? Can nothing stop us thinking nothing can stop us thinking? What good's a good voice if your tunes are bad?

What if the camera jams? Isn't there more vinegar? Which were the pages you ripped from the book? Isn't there another way out of the kitchen? Is whimsy worse than wordlessness? What's holding us back?

There was from March 3rd to April 3rd the appearance of reality

'Remarkable Report by Some Poetic Agents', W.S. Graham

L.M. Kilbride

I Plant the Seed Within Myself

I plant the seed within myself –
a burial with the logic of a dream.
My right hand perished in the act itself.

The last birds long since scrabbling in the dusk
for wild oats left and sang the evening home.
Against the dreamperfect nameless husk

I wake, pray, write, we see our friends and pain
comes empty-handed back to bed and sleep;
no earth no sun no wind no rain

can fail to gather in one self
no more or less than who we were.
I plant the seed within myself.

Richard Price

Are You Still There?

Are you still there? –
The sea is talking in its sleep,
fond names, and no blame each.
The sea would crush you, but you keep it in reach.

Are you still there? –
The sea is singing in its sleep,
hard tunes, song ground from speech.
The sea would punish you, but you think it's here to teach.

Not every question sees the light on the hill.
Not every question gleans the spoil from the spill.
Do you think a question will keep the waves still?
(If your question won't, no one else's will.)

I'm alone here, surrounded
                    by people I'm told I know.
I want to be closer – proximity
                  is touch and go.
Language is lethargic, affection – just won't show.
I need your presence, your delicate lessons,
        your yes to yes, your intricate no. Are you still there?
Could you let me know?

Are you still there? –
The sea is turning in its sleep,
stone dreams and bodies on the beach.
The sea would crush you, but you keep it in reach.

Hannah Lowe

River

I dreamt of living in a boat on the river
like once I'd seen: a marina behind the town
with oaks and greenstone sculptures, the soft mirror
of water, and nesting between two boats, a swan.
But when I returned, there were no swans or oaks,
just miles of coloured boats, their rusted flanks
colliding, and the breeze stank and the water choked
with rats, where children dipped their cans and drank.

And in one cabin window, I saw my mother,
her mouth the shape of my name, and in another,
I saw my son, his face pressed to the pane,
a yellow car in his palm. And the wild sky rained
its horrible rain. And on the riverside
my father stood and hugged his bones and cried.

Paul Henry

Violin Tide

And this is the sea, of course
scrawling by moonlight in its room,
not quite getting the line right
where it meets the shore.

The earliest hours still find me
thinking of you; somnolent tides
rise towards daylight.
Perhaps you have drowned in me.

A table lamp shines the grain
of an old violin in the grate
and down the slope from your dreams
the bay similarly shines.

Perhaps you are not so far away
from the moon in the violin
and the clock I should wind, to hear
the workings of the bay.

At least in your dreams
see how I cannot get this line
to make sense of the sand,
and how I am running out of time

and how easily the night and the day
exchange places, the land and the sea.

Ronnie Duncan

For W.S. Graham

(1978)

Sydney, I dreamed this morning you had done something
Terrible like dying and I awoke not to
Relief only but to trying to sort things out.
Haven't our friends been much depleted lately?
And you dear Master speaking for the rest of us
But also for all of us, have summoned to live again
And in your language tender, violent Roger,
Abundant Bryan, uneasy, lovable Peter.
Yet not these friends only, not your father even
Turning to speak perhaps something as he leaves
(You note I catch your dialect) not these loved
Ones ultimately but the lived language alone
Must bear that resonance of grief and love.
Sometimes I wake in fear in the small hours
Listening for the sound of breathing. Reassured,
I see before drifting back the candle burning
In far-off Madron. I know you are keeping watch.
What price your vigil? O unsleeping guardian,
Revealer of what one dare not face, grappler
With aloneness, gives us a bear hug across the shires,
Bring close your suffering Celtic face with the fierce
Brows poised to say something although you do not speak.
Dawn lights blue chips of glass in Madron's window.
Rooks relieve the vigil. And yet you still
Keep tapping across the silence. Watch it, my dear,
Do not desert the keys too soon. Besides,
Who else would keep watch over us in the small hours?

What shape of words shall put its arms
Round us for more than pleasure?

'What is the Language Using Us For?', W.S. Graham

Douglas Dunn

"One Renfrewshire Man to Another"

(W.S.G.)

To articulate clearly what is difficult to say
I shall transmit this by a beam from a lighthouse
Over the eventful, unforgiving waters
Across many a headland and many a bay.

Edwin Morgan

[*Verse letter dated 29 October 1950*]

To Sydney in Truro Ward, this dark Sunday evening
In a little frost, in a little fog, a verseletter.
– Nearly a month since I wrote you, and yes after
Promising better, but I am bitterly constrained
With lectures and work and the books growling around me
Hated, here, hellhounds, as I write: forgive me.
And first, how are you far away in that hospital?
Do you mend, and are you drugged still, can you
Hold a pencil yet for makarwork, for trobar
Close or frank? I am anxious to hear
And hope by this time you will have good news
I mend but slowly, it is an end that only
Will mend slowly! and I am sick of the discomfort
And the sour patience of a poor inactivity
But both should end soon. It is the poem
That has suffered, and its inactivity is
My main restlessness. Come back time and energy
And Christmas weeks come on, animators
Suspended, men not at work, till then!
(It was verse you requested, dear Joke Grim
From your Zennorward eyrie, and on eagle-wings,
Inked with inveigle-beak, immetriculable
Universe here like the sure iceman cometh –
Hereward Comesnatch Everyballadry.)

O it was gratitude welled for the verse of
Your letter when you said what I had confessed
Could make no difference to how you regarded me,
And if all the imagery and congestion and turgidity
Round a simple thing could have been swept away
I would have swept it away, but it is hard, hard,
To say the simple things that involve a life and a friend,
And to me friendship is like others' love,
The most of life: and for this called, in pain 'love'.

Aberration draws on rebuff, rebuke, contempt.
At thirty one has built a shell, or been beaten.
The shell is complex to guard a simplicity
Or hard to guard a reproved gentleness.
In penalty, sometimes like a live thing
Feeling unaccountable or at sight of a boy's face
In a city street stirs in me crying or
Trying rather to cry and to stretch outward
In a gesture twisting and bursting with yearning:

And I almost then stretch out my own hands
To the boy or the goading vision – almost speak;
Well, you might almost hear it, like sea's singing.
– It is only love trying to wail to be born,
The wailing of the never to be born.
If there are Hesperides, it is not heard there.
Wheesht, sleek silkie, wheesht in the Hert-Hebrides!
– You see how the images come, even here.
I rebuke their aberrant apparition.

You ask about the phrase of my 'friend in golden fell'.
It is one with whom I was naked and whose hair
And down were golden like a coat or fell
Or so exaggerated and word-romanticized
Since his was the golden hair in the dark and the
Down was compounded to him from a noonday
Recollection of a soldier at the beach in Haifa
Gold-felled like the Georgian epic hero
'The knight with the tiger's fell', for whom too I fell.

These things should be in prose (if this is verse)
But never mind; young men as well as old
Must be explorers. (And you must tell me
About the 'Morven maiden' and the 'limekiln Shony' – remember?

A few items, a long time back, I still want to know!)
'Cinderfall'? Well, not exactly a dream
But a halfawake full-imagination (fool imagination)
Nightmare one midnight as I watched the cinders fall.

Where now again they fall, inexpressible hour
Of the heart, when the sinking log hisses and the coal
With its faint crackle feeds the waning glow!
It will soon be twelve, and in the firelight darkness
I sit finishing fashioning this pyrotechnic
Glasgow-to-Cornwall Very-light, a Halloween
Hallowed Catherine-Wheel, a rocket of remembrance
And a poor aurora of northern thanks,
And send it all up, to flash for an hour on your sickness.

Andrew McNeillie

Night-Snow

wee song for Sydney Graham

The real poem never ends.
The blizzard beneath its last footprint
is where we search in its memory,
the blizzard that is also night
as fresh on your face as snow.

Night-snow the ultimate
a body must weather, body I say,
but I mean soul
out on the manhole sea
where the littoral-minded sail

beyond Cape Metaphor to be.
And Sydney Coastguard keeps his watch
ticking on course for Greenock,
with Alfred Wallis at the wheel
aboard the good wreck *Alba*.

For who but a blind one can't see
Scotland from Cornwall? –
every small hour of the year
with the heart in the right direction
and a glass to his eye.

Lesley Harrison

Ilulissat

'Outside
    outside myself
        there is a world
he rumbled, subject to my incursions'
    Paterson, William Carlos Williams

I

impossible.

sterile extrusion
the rigour of its beauty

its crumpled geometry
worked to defeat.

light, stopped.

locked in its form
shuttered and windless

in dry rifts,
split, furrowed, mottled, creased.

II

trundling
bulging from behind,

its too heavy body
its natural carapace

shelving green,
sinking the sea beneath it

the difficulty piling up,
rising to the surface.

III

swirling backward
on blue flowering currents

rolling up
sudden, in spray and mist

– like the turning of a page
that leaves us blinded for a second –

unlocked in a milky scum
half hid, long on its axis

growing open wounds
of violet, emerald, silver.

a point of astonishment.
lapses of silence.   air.

Alexander Hutchison

Setting the Time Aside

'the sea is not salt enough'

1

Gently, gently gets
things going, as you
well know, and here's
the nub: the dust is up
afresh, and won't come
down till this is done.

Sydney, it's midnight
or shortly after, and I'm
trying to get you framed
in the shot: fixed plumb
in the cross-hair snap.

You're sat in a chair
before a desk, leaning
slightly towards me.
Window edge in;
brick wall behind.

You're puzzled or costive
ticked or cheesed off –
it's a bit hard to judge.
I'll have to take care
to get this straight:
not strain too long
nor squeeze a little tight.

Unlock the gate and let
us in. Unslip the leash

and let the beastie go.
Whatever you've got
to say to me, you'd
better say it now.
I'm all ears.

Would an upright man
betray his father?

Who broke the jade?

Who let the wild
buffalo down?

Surely to death we can offer
up some kind of an answer.

What are we meant
to be? What are we
meant to do? I'm
serious, now, Sydney,
we're starting to get through.

2

Five to the hour as
the long hand sweeps
round. What a puzzler
you've set out for
everybody. We've all
been tongue-tied
waiting for it too.

So where's the gap
or slap, or intersection,
which thresh-hold have
we set our toes to
transgress tonight?

(Hold on a bit, is
that the children starting
up? I think I hear
them through the wall.)

Sydney, Sydney, what happened
in the Pass of Glencoe?

Aye, to you I mean.
All that 'wiry, white-fiery
and whirlwind-swivelled snow.'

What did you mean
and what did it mean
tell me to come back?

3

Kenspeck, kenspeckle:
by means or dint of this
you may detect what
a rascal I actually am.

We ought to be able
to take enough out
now to bank the fire,
get paraffin and candles
in for winter.

Never mind the fact
this looks like an office
in a business block
or some old language
cell waiting to be
demolished. Unclench.
Sing out. 'The tatties
are ower the side.'

What a laugh we used to have.

I'll give you a hand
if that's what you require.

You were never
one for writing 'too
much out of vanity' or
suppressing information
from neglect or disdain.

You always wanted
someone else to hear
it and tell it to.

Willie (chord change) I'm
singing as hard as I can.

I never heard the herrings
come home. I never sought
the sea in that way, no –
though I sought it right enough.

4

That's gone one:
it must be – and we've
still not come (though
it's moving on now) to
a song that wrecks the heart.

I am a man upon
the land; I am a silkie
in the sea. Nobody's
actually headed
that I can tell, without
any door provided.

Just you and that expression
of bricked-in pugnacity.

What leads to turbulence?

Who would you tap
to see if they're sound?

I envy you that
glacier calving: 'its
sudden momentary thunder.'

I saw one once
in Disko Bay
beneath the DC7
stretch, mid-flight.

Full lunar eclipse
the self-same night.

5

Stirring, unstirring
the heavens complete
their happy slow rotation.

Ling and harebell: pinkest
pink and lightest fairest
blue on summer braes
shall still surround us.

6

Listen, that story about
the heilan shepherd does
not ring right to me.

And it's not that your words
are not yet come in to
their own true selves.
They have, or will do.

I *can* sing, by the way, I
said before – though
maybe not now.

I can dance.
(I swear to God).

Whatever you decide
to settle for, whatever
you take our mettle for,
whatever you use
that *kettle* for, we
like you nonetheless.

And there's bound to be
a way round somewhere.

Say the word 'dark'
often enough with clear
intensity. Ears and items
rapidly adjust. Cones
and eye-rods sharp adapt:
light quick quiver.

Fire and reset;
reset to fire again.

Who would you tap?

And who would you
shield from harm?

7

You can just see the chop
on the water. Look over
the side and down.

Let's be nice to the pilot
though he seems to know fuck all.

Be nice. We're yawing
just a little bit.

At least no hydrocarbons
dumped on the tundra;

no frozen shit, nor
chicken dinners neither.

Elsewhere, things align.
Here's mebbe something to chew.
Shoo the crumbs off the table.

'The way is always there,'
says Kung Fu Tsu –
'it's the will that's wanting.'

Who gives a flying
fart (forgive me),
generous master? And, no
I don't think I can lend
you a couple of quid –
if that's what you are
leaning over to ask.

8

Bong-a-long, the clock
once more. Where were we?

The calving. Two
million tons of ice,
gravel, pockets of bacterial
decay: dropping like a
bomb in choppy water
deep down dark
in Disko Bay.

Always you knew
how to lower the tone
to a carrying whisper.

Saying, unsaying
the silence, the gentle
moon comes through
a break of cloud over
Clyde mouth and the Kyles
of Bute, stretching away to
Zennor and Gurnard's Head.

9

Is that you there
yourself, caught on the hop
at the top of the Hope Street
stair? I see your face just
past the gas mantle,

taken up in some
grumpy divination.

Mantle glow or not
I'd recognize you.

That quiff, the growl
the gravel and shine once more.

I've got you now.
I might have known.

And look: the night's a pup.
The day will find us sound.
No flash (no need), no
word, no exit wound.

Having waited, having
wanted, here I am for
you now as sure as fate
as death as taxes all up
front and hot to trot.

10

Firing and unfiring
the shallows, a low sough
of wind from offshore
raises dust on the steps
as we go down: wading
in again to meet the salt
dark lance of the sea.

Somewhere our belonging particles
Believe in us. If only we could find them

'Implements in Their Places', W.S. Graham

W.S. Graham

[Thirty-six Implements]

I have left my place to come to speak
To you. Now from this other place
Inhabited by the very beast
I brace myself to speak with good
Tone that will carry. I love you.
How does that sound? I was only testing.

*

Don't make a mystery mountain out
Of a little hill of sudden affection.
I am no mole. You are no mountain
Ear as we try to get ready
To get together. After all
We meet here on the plains of verse.

*

All language is prison jargon.
You realise I have to believe
A real message can get through.

*

Outside the window of the world
The midges dance above a bush
Making a complex music holding
A language for which there is no key.
That they are dancing there helps us
To communicate even in the negative.

*

O may I ask is Time
Having us on?

                    *

I am here very much at four
A.M. Am I in a deeper night
Than you whose eyeballs observe terrible
Encounters under your dream's hill?
I am only still up out of sleep
Trying to burnish an implement
With my mind's elbow grease to pack
In English and send off to you
For you to put on the mantlepiece.

                    *

Younger my brash prison of joy
Seemed to do me well enough.
Now made modern with its new
Benefits of experience
I can hardly catch a glimpse
Of that young sun and treetop.
My cell's window has risen too high.

                    *

Who murmurs me their secret name?
Is it you? If you could do that
You certainly would be better than me.
Who I am, the name I hunt
After has so far escaped me.
The grammarsow or the waving rook
Surely must think of me as somebody.

*

Is who's listening who I guess
It is? My dear it is so long
Since I held your heart near.
I wanted just to speak but now
Hearing your little ear I know
So well near me I am put off.
Anyhow I was only going to try
To assail some aspect of Reality.

*

Time's not funny enough to dash
My hopes. I go in wide open
To deal with the little team of tenses
To try to win myself a stopped
Place for an instant while I think.

*

This is a book. It is blue.
Those are pages. They are black and white.
That is a famous man. The worms
Do not know his name or colour.

*

Then I myself am more or less
Thought by myself into an exile
Any emperor I could construct
Could cruelly never have put me in.

*

My wings. My sticky legs. I wasn't
Fast enough. My life is listening to
A song wherein I feature about how
My life is stilled, pent in amber.

*

To reduce a word to silence is just
As creative as making it say something.

*

They rush they falter slip and slide
Back under into the oncoming next
Wave as it rears to fold and crash
Land dazzlingly on the early shore.

*

Slaughter my house for pleasure, no
Deardaughter mine as the years the waves
Come in on the island's west shore.
From the off season I can see
The season was busy. The land sharks
Carved up the boeuf de Sassenach.

*

Electric blue dragon showing
Between the high sailing cirrus,
You ask me if I have read your work.
Yesterday in the high bracken
With Mary Robertson looking up
I read it or your brother's work
As you went into another sky.

*

Ben Narnain was a love of mine,
Going up beside the Soordook Burn
And bracken and bog myrtle. The water
Ouzel dipped at the pools. The twite
The mountain linnet caught the eye.
From the top I saw the sword of the long
Loch lying in its scabbard of hills.

*

Not that I thought I owned you but
I hope that lover you have now
You tell me is much more your sort
Finds my fingerprints on your heart.

*

The blemish is this, I think, I could
I would have if I had known
I really could but me knowing
It maybe too well was not sure
What it was I could and the words
Were all against me and would not help.

*

One word. Two word. Three word. Four.
Five word. Six word. Seven word more.
Malcolm Hector MacDonald Mooney,
YOU   ARE   OUT.

*

Brigit. Brigit, I wish you would come down
From the Big House. The tide is trickling out
From the upper pools and as I walk my bare
Footprints fill and cave in. I wonder
Am I too old am I too early here?

*

Illmannered Muse, or maybe only
Muse of foreign manners, could I
I mean could we play together after
All I've said against you? Look,
My dear, come sit on the chair with me.
I have a new dictionary but anyhow
Your words are always terribly new.

*

Boris Karloff's gaed awa'
Tae turn his bolted head tae the wa'.
Mary Wollstonecraft will cuddle
His nut and in the grave they'll huddle.

*

Dodging the Geddes stool.
Scotland leaping dancing
Under the Castle's floodlights
For only at the most
A dram or two of the stuff.
The bailly bawls. The provost proves
The siller-source is sin.
John knocks. Rabbie burns.
At least they were doing something.

*

O Ossian unsigned. O
Unbar Dunbar Scotland's greatest
Man of the Winter and the unkempt
Timbre from the less than formed
Kingdom above the delinquents.

*

Ah Amadeus turning over
In the listening silence of the grave,
Tell me now what music you think
You hear in the wires of the world.

*

Not that it is important to beat
Whoever they ALL are. The best all
Turn over in their graves of art
Hoping (Or maybe they know.) they know
What is going on. Or how their stuff
Is being disturbed to make a new thing.
Even outside my medium I would like
Someone like Mozart to have an affection for me.

*

Listening through the microscopes of power
I heard a rebec under an olive
Sing to me that certainly
My wife would leave me and go down
To live on the prose plains again.

*

It is your shot. What shall you say?
I am waiting? Don't let me put
You off. Is that hair your own?
Piss in the street and language
Crowds on us to slight us.
Cheerio. You're one of the best I've met.

*

This is (Or surely a poem should be.)
A commonplace made with some
Pleasure however we stretch the word.
It is not a visual poem. It has nearly
No sounds you might think of it speaking
About. Neither hot or cold.
Its sensual impact is almost nothing.
Or would you like a bird or a beast
Put in? Right. The furry ears
Of a tameless catamount just show
Over the bank of this last line.

*

I have been pecked I have been gutted
By the raven in whose Trojan
Horse the Muse directs Graham
Operations. Now I lie dying
At nightfall under the rook-loud wood.

*

There's nothing wrong with it except
It takes tantrums and loses heart
Or gains speed and great height
And makes a fool of Der Doppelgänger.
You understand what has to be done?
Look inside and operate.
Maybe it just doesn't like me.
We still have our guarantee.

*

Ideosyncracies of the way
We speak eventually become
Currency and only by Art
Skip the expanded chest of rhetoric
To speak nearly from one to another.

*

I am only beginning I say as I die.
(Not meaning a life to come.) Only
That we die forward as we die back.

*

Do not allow me to sink, I said
To a top floating ribbon of kelp.
As I was lifted on each wave
And made to slide into the vale
I wanted not to drown. I wanted
To make it all right with my dear,
To tell my cat I'll be away,
To have them destroyed, the poems
Which were not objects enough on their own
Even entertainment value. I wanted
Through my saltwater breath to leave
A bubble or two in its abstract sphere
On the surface of their delicious minds.

Corridors have their character. I know well
The ring of government boots on our concrete

'Clusters Travelling Out', W.S. Graham

Linda Kemp

Silent Coast

each waking in the
ear central
so story it
& wide

these that profit
dip &
those that
dip into worlds

so solid
sorry
these words
sold to salt

Tim Atkins

Venceremos! Parra! Huidobro!

Hoy nos hacemos cruces preguntando

Ha llegado la hora de retirase

Ahora comienzo a sacarme el sweater

Estoy triste no tengo que comer

Las magicas gallinas en su planeta allegre!

El metepiedras en el infinito!

La noche ha degado noche en mis cabellos

Tiempo perdido miserablemente!

Funerales No!

Hay que volver a cocinar a lena

Siete miradas para prolonger la vida de la novia

Cuando ella llegaba dejaba una parte mas hermosa

La cordillera Andina

El ultimo rey

Magneticas palabras

Viejos verdes

Muerte Si!

Contra la poesia dirigidia

Este es nuestro mensaje

Para asustar al pequeno burgues

Desde el arco iris hasta el culo

Inolvidables personages sagrados

Today we cross ourselves wondering why

The time has come to go!

I start to get out of my sweater!

Sad because I have nothing to eat!

The magic chickens on their happy planet!

The meteorocks in the infinite!

The night has left night in my hair!

What a miserable waste of time!

Funerals! Hell, No!

Let's go back to cooking with wood!

Seven glances to prolong the life of the bride!

When she got here one lovely part!

The Andes!

The last king!

Magnetic words!

Old swingers!

Death! Hell, Yes!

Against the poetry of purpose!

This is our message!

To frighten the petit bourgeoise!

All the way from the rainbow to the asshole!

Unforgettable holy mothers!

Jane Goldman

Everything SOLID

'The School House, Yarrow, Scotland was made for pregnant Rams – everything SOLID; Joy
enters Selkirk each morning just as, I imagine, the first Churchill Tank entered Berlin. Anyway,
she packs up [...] six working days from now, so she will be able to wander about the fields &
bulldoze a few dry stone walls down. She's 'Ooge mon 'Ooge. Glorious thing to paint though.
[...] Dear Aunt Agatha, Is there such a thing as a female Ram. Worried. Tickle my chin with
an Aries? [...] Joy has asked me to tell you as it may be of some remote interest that she has
introduced a form of script writing to her 7 year olds – left handed & half blind you can
imagine the chaos – when the kids can't even spell proper! I look forward to hearing
from you. [...] Is anyone there?'
Letter to Peter Evans, 11th February 1960, Robert Vincent Goldman

All that is solid (Selkirk too) melts
into air it's true but salty marks
still leave a stain and yes now Daddy
why shouldn't I add just for the record
I do too imagine the chaos the worry
decapitating corrie-fisted blind-sided Joy
tank-solid rammed to a bare margin left
heavy with infantry heavy with infantry
a Trojan horse of a Trojan horse
(that's analogy and metaphor for you for you)
emptied out of its no-one here yet here yet
(   ) the space that is before me
that is before you knew it was me before you
and I was almost the adored dehors of your D
never quite to be your anyone there when
I do still still will giggle every time I see it
that facile I of yours trail its bounding line
a descender for an ascender for a possible b
it coasts the fat blank land of the D that brackets
off your right ear snug your right ear opens brackets
to your left ear corralled to enclose eyes nose
mouth a full set (congratulations) your cocked
quiffed stubble-chinned angle-poised lamp head
cupped at the tupped ram's distended blank belly

stalk-necked standing on your five-fingered right
hand anchored so very dexterously starred
it drew itself bravo fatal inches from where the natal
track has crushed her tiny shoes: Is anyone there?
Get up off your knees and listen hard Daddy:
No one (not even you) gets outside the D.

David Briggs

Five Lessons

After W.S. Graham

I

So, Karl, you know my reputation
and you come seeking to master the guitar.
I haven't invited you to sit. Stand
at the window, there, and sing what you see.
If we're to spend the time fruitfully
I must ascertain not so much the dexterity
of your fingers as the clarity of your vision.
Sing, I said. And make it the tune
of what's out there in the street,
not the tired strains of your callow mind's
incessant and predictable soundscape.
Sing me the fleas on the homeless soldier's dog,
the flagging ennui of shopworkers,
acidic graffiti, moss in the windowrubber
of abandoned cars. Sing
just one thing true,
and we'll begin.

I know you're keen to demonstrate your skill,
Karl, but let's return briefly to first principles.
Consider the way a note vibrates in air.
To pluck this string, here,
is to discompose the air around it,
and why should we wish to do that
unless we are certain the disruption we intend
will move all those within its range
to weep like a hit-and-run driver
in the immediate, whisky-wet aftermath.
Your first note is the first word
of your manifesto, the first brick
through the window of Parliament.
It requires not only a sure grip,
but absolute dedication
to the conscious disturbance of air.

III

In this, your third lesson,
I should like you to compare the bars
of this lacquered fretboard
to Jacob's ladder as seen by Milton's Satan
from the purlieus of Chaos, at the edge
of created space. See how my fingers
scale the rungs like angelic messengers
between worlds. It's not enough, Karl,
simply to position your fingertips;
they must be always moving with the graceful precision
of Raphael on God's stairwell, earthbound
to warn Adam of the precarious nature
of his as yet unfathomed condition.
You may practise without picking
while I finish this letter to my patron.

IV

As I have explained, Karl, a chord
is a pattern of waves lapping
against the ear, and to conjure it
we must become both wind and seabed,
and the fetch between continents.
Do not return till you have learned
to sound each chord so true
your audience swears it hears seabirds
between each root and minor third,
till they speak of feeling salt-spray
spit through each perfect fifth.

146

V

Karl, it is good to see progress,
but I believe we've reached an impasse.
I have known for some time I must say this.
Your position in society
is a near insurmountable impediment
to absolute mastery of the guitar.
You fit too comfortably in a world
designed by and for people largely like you.
This is to say, for all your burgeoning skill
you lack grit. You play competently,
without soul, and I fear
our time together has run its course.
Should you commit to a precarious life
of uncertain means, in pursuit of your art,
you may, in time, accrue enough of suffering
to supply the present deficiency.
This is your choice. I cannot say.
Please leave today's fee on the bureau, there.
I trust you understand me when I wish you
nothing but heartbreak, injustice,
ignominy and pain.

Andrea Brady

'Burned in this element to the bare bone'

'Seven Letters', W.S. Graham

Younger in tenements and frothing
at the edge where the sea falls, you are walking
or climbing down or lying
in the dark where you turn
into a fossil or a wreck. The tenement
is a holding turned into property,
the night lies on its outside until it is lit
and broken, what was austere
become a lavish candle of the living
worth approximately £5,000 to any council.

      The eldest turn
      your face to the wall, finishing the air,
      growing up so high
      in a pigeonhole or warren
      all the children go out,
      Isaac Paulos not expected.
      Fie, fie, fie for shame
      turn your face to the wall again.

Yes cry if you can, the night is hammered
by water which rises short
of where it is needed and falls back, alarmed,
the sound of its falling and what is not
a screaming gull. Mark his
chin down, his puny gear not the limit
of his strength, he rushes out and back
like the waves of heat but exorable,
in his humble ear the voice
asking why you left him. What's he to you?
The terrifying endurance of the heart's
mechanics, and the limits of that engine.

May this pleasant month, now a helmet
of idiocy, standing for
nothing before the pleasures of June. This last
hot day, these bunches of flowers. The sky
temporarily overhead. They could not move
on to a shelter beyond the falling leaves
of plastic, there is nothing for it,
their needless

deaths where these words merge and copy,
shameful filters still burning.

16th June 2017

Ahren Warner

'Into that almost glade'

Into that almost glade, a hut, beyond the hut
black forest, needles dropped from high trees,

a faint, white river restless in the middle distance,
the door an almost mouth gouged between

chiselled shingle walls, a crevice or recess
into which you crawl, between two doors,

overlooking a road in which one journo
holds another journo bleeding out into

the sand, dirt, dry grass, a bullet lodged
for the night, cool air humming

between beech barks, stuttering to find
the dried trunk split like a dried carrot,

like elephant hide, like your heel
fissures and fills with mould, to find

the hole in which, short on gas,
short on men, filth for the shower

now scum running, now bullet splitting bone,
ce trou dans lequel on glisse une grande

langue – yes, uncommon cruelty, yes –
and you hunkered in a bamboo hut

and her running blistered, napalm
ridden, molten skin pooling on sand, dirt,

dry grass in which you lie, eyes fixed
between the slats of a black hut

in which he is, indeed, tied up,
bound to a rafter, wires running

from battery to wired balls, whitened
scrotal flesh where clips meet ball

sack in which they bung your mother
and fling her over into the Weise, Danube,

Vàm Cỏ Đông, Tigris, Rio Grande,
Rio Grande de San Miguel, the sack

in which they bung your mother
again and over again and fling her

over, singing: hour of danger, stern resolve,
wise and temperate harmony.

I heard voices within
The empty lines and tenses

'Letter V', W.S. Graham

Pippa Little

Not Earthed but Longing

In loneliness I send word dropped into a deep place
(or shallow, according to tide, moon, turning),
fraying seam travelled by sea's unravelling
and your boot-span at the sore, silenced rub of it:

dark companion of word-roads never mapped
misty and rain-silenced, there was
the touch of your finger-end imaginary
to mine – not earthed but longing.

You said: *a poet hears nothing back*
but what of the beam from Godrevy,
(a new exhalation every ten seconds
of vowels unsceptical, luminescent)

that turns your stone house lunar yet,
lights the same sea paths silvered by sailors' feet
to follow the vanishing curve of the world,
minds your listening, which is love

imagined into words, weathering and wearing down
star-grit and granite, asking *where are you, where*
and giving an answer only you can taste,
the sea-spit, the whisky and the nicotine of it
sent far from the ark on a frail wing,
wheesht

Tony Lopez

Go Back

1

I'm coming to in Coldharbour Lane –
must have blacked out there walking
or dreaming. Where are you Iain?
Peter, David, Kay, Sally, Sydney, John, where now?
It seems to be some kind of loop.
Brixton Hill, Blenheim Gardens, climbing
over to the windmill, brambles and thickets.
This was most likely a way back from the park.
A scrambled memory, a trauma map or make believe –
something you can't deal with and neither can I
otherwise it would come clear – handwritten,
scratched out and repeatedly tried over.
The wall was made of burnt yellow bricks.
I'm coming into Coldharbour Lane.
Where will it lead me?

2

I'm ready; I've made a space
here on the black untidy table.
I'm holding a good gel pen
in my lumpy sixty-six year
old freckled hand waiting.
Waiting to feel something
anything coming through
and in the mean time care
fully writing these words
in short lines on a squared
holed, glued, paper pad –
just in case there might be

a message from you or
even a message from me
coming back altered
like a fish finder under
the charter boat drifting
over a wreck. We are
just beyond your horizon.
The mist is coming home.
Sometimes I can feel
a quick tug on the line.
You never know what or who
might be on the other side.

3

I walked back through Lambeth from the river
at Vauxhall by MI6, past the Oval
to Electric Avenue, Brixton.
Exiled Luis and Eloisa lived there
high above the shops and market stalls
with their eight children.

Was it in Lambert Road or Blenheim Gardens?
My brother David's arm bent the wrong way
on the bombsite – a big hump of rubble
and loose fence over the hiding spaces
fought for with sticks and stones but held
for a brief time only. I thought there would
be trouble when we got home at last.

I walked back to see where we came from
so long after. It is something to remember.

Peter Manson

To Peter Manson

(via WSG)

There are no words
for a knock to encode,
only hearsay, the voice
first my mother's,
now mine, and the photos.
Slender man in khaki
can't colonise my dreams
now, though I still see
that face made up from jungle
foliage behind you,
a forkbeard, hung by the neck.

I had to ask
what you looked like
when not eighteen,
so here you are, turning
away in colour,
my half-silvered mirror
no wiser.
I had to ask
what I looked like
when not eighteen,
what do I look like, dad?

I still can't see us:
the photo is as blurred
as if I had taken it.
The spirit duplicator
cranked a new Manson out,
and you say
to the newborn,
I am:
I hear nothing
but lo, I was, twice
and there are no words.

Stephen Emmerson

Haunted Water

Listen. Put on Morning
Under the sugar docks
The ear the answer
Elements of nature

That firewood pale with salt
Fell and girded me with voice

Very gently struck
Ground down with likely full
Now within the dead
In times of grace
They speak to me in faintest breath

My needs in light more gendered
As certain as a sign falling
Then suddenly all points unfix

The air bunches
& sails me away from home
Treachery becomes me
The shot and spray
That forms a breaking sea

All forms of rest
At this place
Lie down and be mad
Far out, lightly sad
My sides autopsied
In seven letters

Welcome, anytime
Welcome, then farewell
Through the night
And through silence in my mind
Worn to a stop
Its shoal attending time
Lowers into book mould

Listen

What slides between the waving?
Curling a cry for sleeps neck
Quick. Forget.
Make the sign of listening

Amy Key

How Do You Feel About Me Being Gone Forever?

You asked & my mind was on remedies –
sleep, sea, soup, soothe me, soothe me;
the possibility of nerves given up to the sea.
I made symbols of The City Pride, Mary
Margaret O'Hara's 'To Cry About'. My nerves
diluted by the sea, unpacking myself of you.
My weltering nerves as prodigious efficiency;
elsewhere I was performing. I was in retreat,
I couldn't soothe you. My needs: the queasy
comfort of leaving and not being left. My unmet
needs – a conversation. You told me I *used to*
lie down in fields of speedwells as an adolescent. I thought
'speedwells' were made up in your stupor world.
I thought: 'adolescent' is a strange self-identifier.
I made symbols of: chop suey, Chelsey's BAD BAD.
I reasoned with everyone: this isn't a sustainable
way to love somebody, my nerves stapled down
by list-making. Things I was scared I did not know
(song to be played at your funeral). Things I did not
want to know (your unmet ambitions). I made symbols
of 2L of cider, Heavenly's 'Three Star Compartment'.
In my garden I noticed speedwells had already taken
root. I couldn't pay enough attention. The cat's face
became a symbol. My grief burned out before its time –
                              nerves a wall I leant on.

Gently disintegrate me
Said nothing at all

'Enter a Cloud', W.S. Graham

Lindsey Shields Waters

The Beyst in the Spais

Shutt upp. Shutt upp. Thair's no bodie heyr.
If ȝow thynk ȝow heir sum bodie knokyn
On the othir syde of the wordis, pey
No attentioun. It will be onlye
The grete creator that thumpis its taylle
On silens on the othir syde.
If ȝow do nocht even heir that
I'll gyf the beyst a quik skelpe
An thruch Art ȝow'll heir it ȝelp.

The beyst that lyffs on silens takis
Its byte oute of ethyr syde.
It pads an sniffs betwisht vs. Nowe
It cumis an lapis my meaning vp.
Caw it ower. Caw it across
This curiows necessarie spais.
Get off, ȝow terribyll inhabetar
Of silens. I'll nocht hav it. Get
Away ti quhoevyr it is wyll hav ȝow.

He's goyn an if he's goyn ti ȝow
That's fayr eneuch. For on this syde
Of the wordis it's lait. The hevye moeth
Bangis on the pane. The quhol hus
Is slepyng an I remebyr
I am nocht heyr, onlye the spais
I sent the terribyll beyst across.
Watche! He bytes. Lysten gentilly
Ti any sang he snorts or growls
An gyf hym fude. He means neyther
Wele or yll towartis ȝow. Abufe
All, shutt upp. Gyf hym ȝowr lufe.

David Kinloch

A Vision of W.S. Graham's Hippopotamus in Venice

'Each word is but a longing
Set out to break from a difficult home.'
'The Nightfishing', W.S. Graham

What Graham heard first
Was the matronly chafe
Of her widow udders
On the Algonquin Hotel's
Thick pile; what he saw

Was the swing and the
Prance of her all-
Belly, softer and more velvet
Than the empty, numbered
Corridor; what he sent,

Swimming across Iapetus,
Was this old sea-cow
Now wellingtoned
In Venetian shallows
As real as yellow
Café chairs rafting
Marble and meltwater.

Hippo moons at Byzantine
Domes seeking us
Out of the crowd.
And I pray that – gingerly –
She'll not step up
Onto duckboards
And mince our way…
But she does
And the city sinks at last.

I am lagooned in silence
Until the lapping torches
Nuzzling Palazzi stairs dive
Down like bell anemone
And phosphoresce the green.

And then through the flood
I hear the slightly panicked
Whirr of castagnetting hippo
Feet as they lose their grip
And power churn the water-burn

Down to me: her skirts of flesh
Bulge out, her piggy blue
Mosaic eyes and Pantocrator
Face, benevolent as Mary
Poppins, peer out at me.

She seems to speak
A delicate fossil tongue
And tells me it's the one
Will buoy me up again
And recreate the stones of Venice.

So we dredge the sludge
Of Istrian effluent, dodge
Drowning ducal piles
And make our treasure-chest
Discovery beneath the cemetery isle:

A cache of language
Beneath the Fondamenta,
Waterlogged parchments
Of Scottish glossaries
Plugging the solid caranto:

Here is dull broach of
Lion drenched in a
Summer-sob, there a
Map of *water-gaw*
Where it all began again.

But her hooves crunch over
The corralled etymologies:
Ruined horny graptolites
That only once caught sense
In tiny comb-like sieves.

Here is a stash of *utteridge*
Strewn and *unmensefu*,
The *undersook*
Of 'Sestieri': *a sumphie*
Stour-o'-Words.

There is *maroonjous* pine
That Gritti and Ca Rezzonico
Deliquesce upon, the water-
Slain-moss that peats their roots
And eats their damp-proof stone.

Oh for a *neid-fire*
To ignite canals
Electrify a doge of sound
That would convoke
The glittering, *dowie* signifiers.

I turn in the *wallowa*
Turn to hippo in the *wallowae*,
But she's slipped aloft already,
A 'cathédrale engloutie'
Burbling on her mobile.

I wonder in the *howe-dumb-deid*
Beneath the 'canalazzo'
Wonder at that hoof
Of *umbersorrow* lit
By the lagoon's blue day,
Wonder what my hippo
Is using me for.

Glossary

summer-sob – frequent slight rains in summer; *water-gaw* – the fragment of a rainbow appearing in the horizon; seen in the north or east, a sign of bad weather; *utteridge* – utterance, power of speech; *unmensefu* – disorderly; unbecoming; indiscreet; used of weather: rough, unseasonal; *undersook* – an undercurrent flowing against that on the surface; *sumphie* – stupid, foolish; sulky, sullen; *stour-o'-words* – a wordy discourse; *maroonjous* – harsh, sturdy; *neid-fire* – fire produced from the friction of two pieces of wood; a beacon-fire, also used to express the phosphoric light of rotten wood; *dowie* – sad, mournful, inclined to decay; *wallowa/ae* – an exclamation of sorrow, the devil; *howe-dumb-deid* – used of night, the middle, when silence reigns; *umbersorrow* – surliness, resisting disease or the effects of bad weather.

Nuala Watt

Dear Words

Babble to Scrabble to scat –
who makes decisions on that?

Ritual but not lautir.
Habitual but not lautibah.
Which of you are dictionary-proofed?

Why is table sense
but elbat dennuhs?

Babble to Scrabble to scat –
who makes decisions on that?

When did 'bleh' leap into the language?

What can be caught through amniotic fluid?
Dear green phonemes?
Do you know 'The Jeely Piece Song' from a Hoover?

Parallel.
Parable.
Elbarap.

What is nonsense? What is not?
What is pure linguistic snot?

Efasnu krad esnesnon?

Esnesnon. Esnesnon.

Did I misspell that right?

Babble to Scrabble to scat –
who makes decisions on that?

Alan Halsey

Dear WSG

I thought it might amuse you
now you're on the other side of language
although this probably happened
when you were still on this –

I was talking to a writing group
about your poem 'The Constructed Space' –
I scalpelled it out sound by sound
not by murder to dissect but to show

how the making of that poem so truly
becomes it – when a voice from the back
protested 'I like poems about waterfalls'.
I might have said it's wordfalls that

cut to the quick but oh I'm sometimes
polite. My anatomy lesson was futile
from the start and who anyway knows
what's now befallen your side of language.

Tim Turnbull

Meanwhile, None of This is Happening

1. Solar Eclipse, Tottenham

On the High Road, life begins to imitate
illustration: the light gets all Edward
Hopper; the citizens acquire a look
of fifties Ditko and, as mauve shadows
creep across the street, open themselves
to the uncanny, shield eyes, gaze skyward,
anticipating, perhaps, the arrival
of Klaatu and his eight-foot foam-rubber
buddy, or some chimeric confection
with horns, heads and crowns in abundance.
The traffic is quite silent, and the Palace
Cathedral walls glow rose and white gold
until overtaken by tenebrose
blues and violets, and the estate agent,
Michael, steps out to join the lookers-on,
and Tom the Butcher, Dawn and Mrs Carter,
and Ed Next-Door, and Mr Pointy Head,
Ventress and Trixie, and it almost seems
that we're about to be saved, taken up
to the sky by benefic intelligences
come from the furthest reaches of the cosmos;
but there's a chill with nothing infinite
about it, and gradually, as if someone
were de-tuning the contrast and saturation,
colour and focus lose clarity, then
play is pressed, normal service resumes
and folk go, abruptly, about their business;
and it was, anyway, twenty years ago:
more from where you're standing.

2. Heavy Snow, Meikle Obney

It is like a temporally aberrant
outlier of the 1960s here,
pungent with spilt diesel and shed cattle,
a wee world in its own continuum,
where heat must be coaxed from damp kindling
and wet slack with congealed paraffin wax
and newspaper sheets; the water runs red
with iron and bubbles up through the kitchen
floor in heavy weather. At night, livestock
break loose and mill senselessly about
the house and cars in approximation
of a disconsolate mob. The hills, grey
and ochre, hunker above us; below,
down the dirt track in Juncus-feathered fields,
stands a mire Grimpen in its lethality.
This morning, though, everything is stilled
by a forearm's depth of snow absorbing
all sound. And it reflects and magnifies
the meagre winter sunlight, so that we
are drawn, after breakfast – for no one,
three miles of road below the Witch's Stone
blocked solid, is going anywhere today –
to gambol and frolic with idiot dog
like children, building coal-eyed and -nippled
snow lady, and fighting and cavorting
in a muffled world at once circumscribed
and, seeing out across the white wide valley
beneath the white unbroken sky, boundless.

3. High Winds, Rosemarkie

August, but a trough in the Atlantic
has twined isobars about itself and hurls
hail and squall across the isle and the firth,
rattling us, here in this tin box, as per
the predictions of Mr Socksanshorts,
battle-hardened caravaneer and sage,
dispenser of heavy duty tent pegs,
which, at least, pinion the ripped awning
to the ground while its inflatable frame
flubbers in the tempest. Hard rain hammers
the misted windscreen and dog grumbles
from driver's seat as we resign to playing
house with toy food and tea brewed in alloy
vessels on minimal gas hob. Outside,
where one might expect cyclonic flotsam –
cows, chickens, men in rowing boats, and barns –
cagouled and battered campers strain their way
to overflowing toilet blocks, and tents
and bits of tents cartwheel along pursued
by weeping owners. Each gust of wind
is stronger than the last and we are braced
to spend forever here, enclosed in pressed
steel and safety glass, watch condensation
drops pool and trickle, feel the air thicken
with CO_2. Wrapped in layers of sleeping
bag, we fail to sleep until just before
dawn and then expire, but when the dog
alarm clock agitates and the sliding door
roars back, the world is where it was again
and sunshine offers its reprieve.

W.N. Herbert

The Nightfishing

after Picasso

1

Way down in the warm blue crevasse
of night its fishing commences as
the boat of millions of fingernails drags
across a blackboard-winged bay.

Across the painted harbour at Antibes
we see a painting of Broughty Castle
in which the back of my father's head is
looking back at me covered in seaweed.

He was the rock from which I threw all
those nude tarnished spoons like the stars
of heaven landing as soft shoe crabs, or as
a spattered dress on the Phibbie Pier.

Olga the cross-legged ballerina and
Dora-Thérèse of the Arse-Parked Bicycle
look on. Two scoops of testicle
are lifted to a scalene tongue.

2

Like a yoyo the old apocalypse comet
twirls from Mrs Picasso's celadon sleeve,
and is shot over the green igloo cheek
of the harbour wall by our common

lust to see through the language, that *origine*
du monde Venn-diagrammed between
night's labia of dreaming and grief –
did you hearsee or saw it beneath

the torches like twists of lemon sweets, with
a fork for our gladiatorial silverware? The quartz
fish records your squint like a stubbled general
under its thumbed-back lid of waters;

it is a word deloused of mere speakers,
naked amid this kelp of ekphrasis,
its etymology more like sleep itself, which
our sloth-faced fisher in the stripy T-shirt

of yamming what he yam
has a stab at. Nightmatters prefer their own
spectrum of purple and olive green, but get
crumpled newspapers of anatomies

in the globe of bluejeans and spinepelt, alpha
boat of wet elbows, nostrils leaving
their own faces in a flare of want,
kill glimpsed through displacement

of krill. Dora's face is slapped by the paint
brush into a doormat of distress above
Thérèse's breasts and genitals brush
stroked into a pyramid dress and a prone heart.

The reticule of light is folded over
the bow as we lose hold on the heat of
the hand of what those we loved knew,
so improvise the retention of ice.

3

From the porthole rubbed in
the restaurant window in the colour-
less predawn my father sips his sage tea,
preparing for this ferry that will slip

beneath the vault of ice as though between
a whale's blue ribs back to that cavewall
of tattoos, back when the word
and the mark and our skin were one.

Beneath the tongues of all the fishes,
the pierwomen claim, is the real name
of his port of call; in one of their bellies,
reply the fishspearers, rests his wedding ring.

Beneath the whalefish eye of a raw sun,
the singing that does not know
it is song; within its lyrics without words,
the word to be that must have loved us.

Sam Buchan-Watts

Lines Following W.S. Graham's Imagined Forest

'I have set you here'

On the way into the woods, do you feel someone
turn the focus of the lens with the topmost parts
of their forefinger and thumb –
in line with the crick of your neck, as you turn to look
but feel the head fixed straight. The branches tick,
someone set them going. The woods set you here,
so as to feel away from thoughts but still you think
I never really entered. The way into the woods is in a way
to go round the woods: the woods are always in the way
when you're in them (if they're woods). The way in weighs
on the memory of summer like a cloak momentarily hung
over the sun. The way in is a process of hyphenation,
like statements about the weather, the weather in the woods.

Ancient of runes the stone-cut voice
Stands invisible on Zennor Hill

'Two Poems on Zennor Hill', W.S. Graham

Matthew Francis

A Dream of Cornwall

i.m. W. S. Graham

1

Now only the sea is ahead of us,
a meniscus of blue, unscratched by waves.
I feel we are driving into an eye.
Sometimes a glassy blip slithering across
makes me wonder if the eye is my own.

2

In the snug under the cliff
where leaves shaped like the ears
of lynxes, elephants, donkeys,
grow in a Max Ernst profusion,
we sweat in the hothouse steam
that reeks of wild garlic.

3

West of Zennor, foxgloves and redhot pokers
incandesce in the rain. The land becomes pinched.
The fields are stone pens for a single cow.
A coach is winding round the lanes towards us.
We can see everywhere, as if we were flying.

4

I stand in the look-out hut
where men watched for the gleam
that meant the fish were returning,
and see the molten shoal
spit and leap on the surface.
There is no one to shout to.

5

A man is typing something in a cottage
by the pilchardy light of an oil lamp.
I am trying to read over his shoulder,
but the page is all consonants and obelisks,
and I am miles away in my childhood.

6

The sea is not yet dark,
a laundered cloth stretched over
the mahogany land,
as the candles of lighthouses
flutter their yellow. Tonight
we'll dine in the ocean.

Moniza Alvi

Motherbird's Bruises

Her bruises can't be seen
beneath her soft feathers.
　　I know they're there.

Once one was exposed –
a mark of violent hues, one shade
　　merging into another.

The roughness of birds.

She would prefer to forget
how she received them.
　　I enter into the heart

of the bruise which carries on
bleeding invisibly –
　　a single spreading

blue-black-dark-sea stain.
I fly straight into a storm cloud's
　　dreadful purple flowering

　　and I take on responsibility

　　　　as if I had caused it.

John Wilkinson

On Goonhilly Downs

to W.S. Graham

Louring from the mantle, granite hum
jacks its column over Land's End,
thick graphite smudges spread
on the fair day's ceiling, slide in layers...

Audible excess, that spheres gobble
on the erupted seabed of Goonhilly...
Inland, sucked chalk throws up spoils
humped above the jalopy cottage

where song was long prepared for such
bonny arrivals: Mostly what's heard
spills off a lap a baby bounces on.
Leave that warm capacious lure;

leave, soft ticking wants to seduce
with its opaque homophony,
entangling with its dulse-red strands
no bolster but a slab of concrete.

Snow constructs its car and high wind
carves a cottage. The cast off
beats at adamant stone:
stricture has confused the compass

swollen like a globe of all directions:
restore the social compass with rough
trestles. The amber not the quartz.
Sudden song belts out on wings

across impossible intervenings,
swooping on air's paving with a rush,
swooping on greased rungs into
the public house, where your plurality

cut time singular to a line of days,
a ridge bouncing a star back vertically...
a pulse, a skipping song or ballad
collects likeness over earth like Sirius.

Such terrible times will never say time.
Reports blather from quartz veins.
Skies scowl, lowering swallows
scrawled in a slow exposure tracery,

criss-crossed, messed up proper,
pluck straw away from globes, downily
lining their nests: Celandines
the stars time-since soon will cluster.

Rachael Allen

Dolmen

Composted tomb
of dusty human.

Was this ever a
stolen girl's grave?

Shed of clumped
and blasted

mysticism. Square
burial blank.

Grot to pray in, or haunt.
The toasted girl

beneath the fallen
down ton weight

capstone, still brushes
her hair in the crackling

gorse, climbs out
with shrunken arms

each night, years pressed
into the moor by blue.

Kelvin Corcoran

Forty-five Lines on W.S. Graham

The house where Graham lived
in Madron in the rain
is a shell of song to a light tenor
longing for Loch Thom.

Next door on Mount View Terrace
a satellite dish suspended
listens to the running streams
make ready the risen speech.

From his house of granite, house of words
the moor is flying blind
the black lane shining at the sky
for Penwith to silence babble.

The granite spiral staircase
from the Madron workhouse refit
lies broken up and buried
in the fields of Graham Land.

Treads worn smooth by the feet of the poor
ascending and descending
in the fields of Graham Land
where poetry takes its turn.

*

The second location of Graham Land can be found
at S 65° W 63°, country code AQ, population zero,
though names are disputed it's there, waiting for your step.

Using dog sleds and a de Havilland Fox Moth
we determined that Graham Land was a peninsula,
a white tenement in an unfixed magnetic field

Half-seen through the interference of the snow;
then the snow becomes the fabric of your breathing
and you hear high voices on the other side of blizzard.

The worst of it was settling down at night alone,
the ice song sounding from the deep sea channels
sets the world atilt roaring at the broken door.

*

The last of Graham Land, *listen back, listen back*,
is the white tenement of memory and the bare language,
the worst of it how the names weather uninhabited
– and this on a day of talk in the green wood of Madron.

And that would be the Graham Reel you join,
as if there ever was a choice, as the brimming tide
breaks in particles belonging as first light on Fore Street
launched even later there becoming a time.

– Do you know a poet called W S Graham lived here?
Yes, I do, there's a plaque up there on the wall – look,
see the day showing its devices, swaying to the sky
and see that large body of water sounding us out.

Launched even later there becoming a time.

John Wedgwood Clarke

Peter Lanyon

I go again to haunt your hand's window
smeared into cloud, star-spatter, night-blue seams,
your wing-juddering, scraped-edge clearing vapour –

Perform me back into shadows, gestures,
paint, a place before its name, lightly suspended over
Atlantic lights, ghost foam, St Just spider mites.

You opened mine adits and I set my fire after you,
running into the shafts, those house swallowers.
You swept me to the edge, the Steeple's definitive snow.

Quartz storms in the granite batholiths, the balding
brain of the land your line ignites, brushstrokes
cleaving the dark, spraining paint until it falls

down the sheer silence at Botallack, death in the failure
of a bolt. All the weight, all the thick green toil
you had to mine your way through opens

the cloud's all angles, self-issuing, into the damp
net-lofts and hiss of propane, the thundering
waves surging up the sand into rust and salted glass.

Speaking to you and not
Knowing if you are there
Is not too difficult.
My words are used to that

'Dear Bryan Wynter', W.S. Graham

W.S. Graham

Lost Somewhere Between Krista and Nicolaos

Not all that lost but certainly
The Greek sun observes me as
A visitor with my Firth of Clyde
Blue eyes from the north and fries
My face to a frazzle. Let me move
And lie down in the olive grove.

I know I am unbeautifully
Lying down among the crushed
Flowers of a foreign country.
The place is beautiful difficult
To fit in even to my vanity's
Own place where everything happens.

Of course I am not lost except
Nobody knows where I am. I am
Only a visitor always. And what
Should I worry about lying here
Looking up through the olive branches.
I don't have to say anything

To anybody. I am going up
To find the village I saw high
Up on the mountain, a faint few specks
Of habitation shining. I lie
Here on my back crushing the flowers
Looking up through the olive branches.

W.S. Graham

[*It is as Though the Very Movement Comes Out of Silence*]

It is as though the very movement comes
Out of silence wanting us to speak.
Of course I mean myself lost wanting
To be taken up by something outside myself
That I can get my doubtful teeth into.
It is so difficult when you find yourself
Late at night when the names of the people are gone
Wondering what you are doing. Or if you acted
In front of them to deserve some respect,
And then at the same time fight hard
To not sit thinking making those people up
In a bad way to help one's own behaviour.

Who is to help me then? Who is to help
Me now in this position of no belief
In myself or anything I have ever done
To try or by accident. OK I get a kick
Out of the fucking verse but so unspeakable
About it's like a cancer threshold pain
Which in its own I can't tell you about.
Yet if somebody asked me are you happy?
I would say yes I am a happy man.
I am a happy man. I hum both day
And night and even in the dream's dazzle
I make poetry from silence. I do not whistle.

I have not met myself and I get worse
At trying to do that. I must hurry up
To catch myself before I go away.
Not that it is interesting to other people
But I am only human and I find
I want some indication of love and respect
From my fellow beasts no matter how different
They seem from me. In unemotional
Despair I put my coat on and go out
On to the empty night-road in the dark.
There are no stars to see. I walk in braille
Tapping my white writing stick on the wall.

To help to speak I clutch this attitude
Of me outside walking. It is as much
Reality as you shall get to because
The words of making it up are far realer
Than you walking with the rain on your face
Tapping hedges and walls with a white stick.
What are you here for? I am here for nothing.
Nothing gives me a hint. I am a great
Constructor of ideas to help me strive
To continue. I even have to ask the hedges
If my stick is white. On my left cheek
The western rain gives my cheek a lick.

W.S. Graham

The Owl

Ho Ho Who Who now in the dark
Obviously I love you wanting
To put a line or two towards you
With no sound. With no sound.

I think you are the most translated
Bird from bird into language.
Circle your head but don't get too
Self-conscious sitting up superior
To the day birds, Speug and Stare
Who are anyhow off asleep.

In this address to you in verse
The dark is mine tonight. It is
A dark which I have manufactured
Myself for me to see you well in.

How do you keep your eyes open
Sitting in the dark on line
Sixteen. It's getting up. Or maybe
I'll meet you in the black wood
Of Madron under your own terms
With a frightened mouse on my head.

W.S. Graham

The Curlew

Curlew, what is to happen to you
Celticly alone flying across
All the moors of my memory?
You need not answer that. You are
Beyond them all. O what a fine
Long neb spears the air before you
When you pass over me lying
And then twist off your course and utter
The curling longing cry. I know
I am using you. Even although
I have suffered from a short nose,
It is not that. I like you anyhow.

If you are crossing, maybe tomorrow,
That freshwater stretch we call
Loch Thom, tell old McClachie
The poetry boy is wanting home.

W.S. Graham

[*As the Tide was Streaming Out*]

So as the tide
Was streaming out
Over the oyster
Catching early
Strand, I stepped over
The clinkered side
Of the half-afloat
Family skiff.
With my bare foot
I pushed us out
In a long glide
Ascending over
The weed and the young
Flounder groves
Of the long loch.

This is Loch Long,
A real place.
Here in the seaweed
Breathing air
It lies between
Its hills still.
My half-cousin
Brigit is with me
Sitting light
On the stern seat.

I dip my dazzling
Blades in
And lean back on
Their spoons of water.
The little whirl
Pools swirl away

From the bite at the end
Of each blade.
Bright drops
From the oars sprinkle
And pock the water
Moving astern
Like a platform
Of travelling silk.
This is a little
Trip of words
Long on the page
Narrow in swathe
Short on time
A glide of words
For three people
On a Gaelic loch.
Yes, you are one
Of the people here.

If it were looking
Down the loch
The eye of The Cobbler
Would see our speck
Of skiff moving
Between the morning
Of the shores.
It would see Brigit
Nod towards me
At the end of each stroke
At the whipend
Of the blade's bite.

Why are we here?
Together? Well
You may ask indeed.
And you, Brigit,
Don't stand up.
Keep the boat trim.

W.S. Graham

Lines for a Poster

O Ludivici, Cheerio.
Halt or be killed. The babes of the grave
Are shouldering arms for what they believe.

Halt. I see you out of the wall,
All flowers walking in a furnace.
Halt says the halter, the Art device.

Halt in the cause of the Future Past.
I see you walking around in the round
Putting your sound with another's sound.

I can hear you. I can see
Through your flat eye of mirror
Your terror touch my own terror.

And in the furnace of their times,
Riding abstract, lonely joys,
Burn the contemporary girls and boys.

Halt or be killed. I perish also
For ever and for ever O.
        O Ludivici, Cheerio.

W.S. Graham

The Answerers

How would you like to ever find
At long last what you really are?

Duck said the flying samovar.
Home said the fighting temeraire.

How would you like to find what
The man who lurks inside is like?

Thai said successioun o kyngrik
Was nocht tae lawer feys lik.

And would you ever like to drop
Into your true self not ready?

You've come a long way said he.
The man you want has gone to sea.

How would you like to find at last
The lost wee girl you have always been?

Don't seek that said her good man
And the tear blinded his een.

How would you like to drop dead
And see yourself from outside?

Aye said the tink o' Gairlochside.
Aye said all the ghosts in the language.

How would you like to ever find
At long last what you really are?

No said the Lady o' Dunbar.
No said the marching Earl o' Mar.

W.S. Graham

[*And Who Will Hold Me in the Dark*]

And who will hold me in the dark
Corner of my life when suddenly
My cheek is touched by the hand
Out of nothing I have been able
To think about before? I fell
On Madron Road under the bramble.

Don't stop. Don't look at me here
As your sidelights sweep across
The midnight hedges. I am lying
Down in my thorny ship to sail
Through the dark rain into all
The confections of the night people.

W.S. Graham

An Entertainment for W.S. Graham for Him Having Reached Sixty-five

What are you going to do
With what is left of yourself
Now among the rustling
Of your maybe best years?
This is not an auto-elegy
With me pouring my heart
Out into where you
Differently stand or sit
On the Epidaurus steps.
What shall I say to myself
Having put myself down
On to a public page?

Where am I going now?
And where are you going
Tricked into reading
Words of my later life?
Let me pretend you are
Roughly of my age.
Are you a boy or a girl?
And what has happened to you?

Look at the chirping various
Leaves of Mr Graham's
Spanking summer. Where are
You at? I know my face
Has changed. My hair has blanched
Into a wrong disguise
Sitting on top of my head.

Beside each other perched
On the Epidaurus steps.
Where am I going to go?
Shall I rise to follow
The thin sound of the goats
Tinkling their bells?

This morning I am ready if you are,
To hear you speaking in your new language

'A Note to the Difficult One', W.S. Graham

Annie Freud

Sydney on the Street of Knives

You, like Hephaestus, fallen and unmothered,
woke from Hope Street Greenock into an olive grove.
As *he* made swords and jewels for the Gods
so *you* took a notebook to see how words behaved.
No bare-breasted mannequins, no leaping acrobats,
nor mythic beast – part-hippopotamus, part-lion –
but instead three men, Elias, Nikos and a boy
at work in their dark shop, forging scrap and iron
into the fabled knives of Crete. No street ever sounded
as italicized as yours. How you enunciate the word
– kn-i-i-i-ves – with rapture unlike any I have heard.
You saw steel sparking on the carborundum wheel
settling an edge onto the tempered blade. Dionysus claimed
you for his own and on his breast your head was laid.

Penelope Shuttle

Mac Lir

Lyonesse is here for the taking
says Manannán mac Lir
old fart of the sea
poking around where the tide
dips and ditters

Just imagine there's no Lyonesse
says he
and a poor soul rocking herself to sleep
in the pain of things
has only the silver blanket of tears for comfort

But there's always Lyonesse
purrs Manannán mac Lir
dirty old god of the sea
stroking the plush of her bones
milking her salty veins
feasting on her DNA
there's always Lyonesse

Paula Bohince

Goldmine

Gold in the black box
      of the stitched-down mouth –

    beyond
the kissed lips, the teeth the tongue
      spoke to, in secret –

    the lips, the gold
remembered and cursed. Overlooked
     at burial time

    and buried. Regret

    as crenellated leaf
over molars. Uprooted: fingertip-small
     burnished tulips.

    Royal twins
enthroned in the stoic jawbone
     for Eternity.

Egyptian princes. Remedy
     of gilt. What heft remains –

    Him
and not him. What shines, what travels
     and what travels no further.

    My traveler, lost father, gift
horse, mine, goldmine.

John Burnside

Fantasia on a Line of W.S. Graham

> 'I leave this at your ear for when you wake,
> A creature in its abstract cage asleep.'

It was summer from here to the coast
all morning, the side door
open to a wind that found me out
so quietly, I barely felt a thing,
a drift of bees, the pigeons on our roof
as casual as the light that slipped indoors
and wandered gradually from room to room,
unravelling the serge and herringbone
from empty winter coats and tangled scarves,
or gilding the lip-balmed rim of the hand-cut glass
you set down on the chimney breast
at midnight, when you turned without a word
and went to bed.

I still remember when I cared enough
to watch you sleep, as if I'd catch a glimpse
of something hidden, something you had loved
in girlhood, or the year before we met.
Now I am scarcely curious enough
to wonder what it is runs through your mind,
or what you think it means, when you unearth
some partial recollection over morning
coffee, some old
motto from your mother's Christmas box,
a skipping rhyme, where everybody dies,
a life-size model of the sacred
ibis you constructed from a book

of chromolithographs, to take the place
of what you couldn't name, but knew

was missing – and this hulk of squandered days
mere aftermath, the business of the house
an epilogue, in which we understand

our only obligation to this world
is not to see how dangerous it is
at first light, when a forced resolve might break
and come to something larger, like the tone
a bell leaves in the bones, after it's gone.
How life persists, for more than pity's sake.

I leave this at your ear for when you wake.

George Mackay Brown

W.S. Graham

Some inmates
may never meet
in the House of Poetry
that has
so many mansions
(and often, alas
the poets
who do meet
– in the webbed corridors
or on stairs looking out on
the apple tree
bare, blossoming, burdened with fruit –
have cold words)
but often
sitting in my northern garret
I have heard
music
from a higher reach
of the House!
The true song
of outpouring mingled waters,
river into ocean
– the heard dark heart –
and under
fish quickening for the net,
and a gull
climbing the Greenock sky,
rivet in beak.

O Greenock, Greenock, I never will
Get back to you…

'The Greenock Dialogues', W.S. Graham

Jackie Kay

Out of the Clyde

'Last home, I crave my ease
stopped for a second dead
out of the speaking flood'
'TO MY MOTHER' from 'Three Letters', W.S. Graham

Since all your steps were taken,
and you'd set off for death,
with your hobnails on Ben Narnain
walking the kyleside shingle.
Since you knew since you were little
you'd return to this young life in death,
to the ship's cradle, the Greenock hills
to the high tenement, your mother's voice,
your father's song, Alastair's homing memory,
you came calmly, puffing light on the page,
to speak for the other side, like an Airlie or a Reid,
fine-tuning your small self, the one you grieved
all your life. Clyde-side clad, you stepped with ease,
not minding yourself on the way, a steady pace, then
stopped – out of the flood – to speak to us,
from the tall tenement of poetry, off on a ship
down the upper Clyde, onto a steamer on the
the Firth of Forth, you carried us, Makar W.S.
– your light lit, your heart light –
all the way down to the love-signed sea,
William Sydney who married Agnes Nessie,
then stood stock still to listen
to your father singing the 'Bonny Earl o' Moray'
a boy once more who learnt the lessons early
that those who hurt you most, you love most dearly.

Robert Crawford

Port

Berth-place of John Galt, birthplace
Of James Watt whose surname named watts,
Slave money over-sweetening your sandstone tenements,
Black GIs from Missouri wowed by your tainted Firth
As they packed railway carriages jammed along long Princes Pier,
Over for D-Day, standing at troop-train windows,
Bemused and smiling to sweet-starved white kids who yelled,
'Any gum, chum?' till packets were thumb-flicked across.
Sea town of the blitzed girl blown upstairs
By high explosives, of the doilied dolls' tea party
Under the kitchen table to a Luftwaffe whistle of bombs
That pause in mid-air while time stops, and dark rings of guns
Round Kirn pound the skies, then the night goes red
With burning whisky, blazing streets napalmed with malt.
Mustering point of mariners, submariners, Jamiesons,
Campbells and seen-it-all, ocean-going clans –
Free French, Poles, Canadians – they line up, assemble, draw breath,
Back-from-the-dead riveters, Stanley Spencered by gantries
At Port Glasgow, teeming from your graveyard shifts
With tools and tool bags, sprucing yourselves up, Comet-
Launcher where the burned-out outdo the living, Cloch-watcher,
Drydock of soft, apocalyptic rain. Through you,
Paradisal dump, persist less the names
Highland Mary, W. S. Graham, or A. Dunn, Bookseller,
Than just the word GREENOCK, its sunstruck, meandering Cut
Incised into Scotland, that thin canal of primroses,
Sunshine and hot walks over the moors to Wemyss Bay,
O slipway of too many ships, battered esplanade,
Your Lyle Road still a panorama of Nirvana,
A hand-stitched prinking of yachts past the Tail of the Bank;
Home to the wee girl whose dad said, 'Tell your teacher
"I'm a MacLean of Duart. We had our own boat at the Flood."'

Only begetter of the Tontine Hotel, godfather of the Atlantic Gulf Stream,
Mother of all voyages out,
Born survivor, bonny fechter, breath
Of fresh, salt air, your people heirs apparent to Popeye
And the *Jeanie Deans*, recession-hit binnacle, druggy
Star port, cosmopolitan with gangways,
Ghost Cunarders and ferries, livewire ready for the ferryman
Whenever he comes, with the summer's day litany of your crossing:
Kirn, Dunoon, Innellan, Rothesay, the Firth of Styx.

Jen Hadfield

The Porcelain Cliff

after The White Road, *Edmund De Waal*

for Aviva

I

When clay makes something for itself
it goes for a cliff just slightly to scale
no leaping carp or calligraphic crane.

No arch of melting cobalt,
no drench of cobalt rain. In a fairy tale,
a boy squeezed a pebble

until it ran milk.
Traverse this snowpack and the details blur
wrists crawling with midges

as you clamber
over its fat, white belly,
treading out the whey.

II

Count to sixty.

Into the opposite of ribs and spurs,
slip crawls secretly.

Dear mud trickles into blind caves,
climbing the growing ladders of itself,
a growth spurt losing momentum.
This is how we entertain our Shadow.

How stone moves in to stake a claim in the valley
a silk invasion, oblique, polite

as the please and thankyou
of stalagmite and stalactite –
until the mould is full as an egg.

III

Is the wind fat with rain? Count fifty
if it comes from the North
with the North's terrible thirst, a prospector's wind
a dry blade whetted
with the scent of walrus.

It licks the mould.
The thirsty plaster sucks up slip.
The clay is fattening the form

soft keys rusting in every lock,
light growing in every shadow.

Now with a Jersey slosh,
milkmaid it into the bucket.

Let the wind lick dry the mould.

Already positive
winces from negative
a thin skin tearing

like a turtle's egg.

IV

The burn runs right off the peat-hill
and under the porcelain cliff.

Even when there hasn't been rain
it runs fast and strong and brown and deep
reliable as a vein

clearing its throat
constantly.

Dust is curious.
Dust is thirsty.

Dust is watching you outside
and in.

It silts your broken tributaries – lifeline and loveline –
wanting to plus up every minus,
clothing your lung-tree with brittle bark,
putting weight on the apples
of your alveoli,

doing what it is made to do
quenching its thirst

filling a form.

v

Dear Foreman,
Thanks for turning the water off. Instead
of swallowing the tapeworm of the snowy M6
I too opened a cave of making with just two little hooks
painted white to keep bad guys
out at night and dreams.

Dentists you scrape and vibrate
the open mouth of the side of the house
Ba Ba Ba Ba Ba A-
MEr-ica singing
in speech like a Northerner, like a silty river 'will you do me a
favour?
gonna get me some nails?'

Two crows peer through the skylight putting me
in mind of audience. A bang like a drum
reveals you're in the hall, calling Hellowww –

Hellowww you've cracked us open like an old lion's mouth
and I have opened something too.

You're carrying bricks, beams, a tune, a joke.
I a pail of slip, heavy as a house.

We are both beginning to make something you
a lion tamer prising
open the old house's jaws.

VI

Clay ties itself
in knots for you.

Pots as thick as a hangover.

Migraine bowls that spin and ring.

Clay has no idea
what it's making.

Innocent of commission,
it knuckles down
to knead itself.

From clay we learn to lose our train of thought
in satin whirlpools' marbling weight
– what was I saying?

with our bare hand
stirring –

VII

The form drops from its mould when it's ripe,
like a fruit faithful

to every damage
done, each scratch a raised scar
each bubblet of air a rash
or pimple.

The impression is faithful.
Bruised like the ur-apple in a golden sleeve of ice.

Smooth plunge into the vortex of the stem
the place it ends and begins again –

crush each like a turtle's egg
melt stone into the milk it's made of.

Jim Carruth

Far Field 3

Here at last – coincidence, freewill –
perhaps you have been sent.
No response required I was not prying
but you do need to know yourself
what works you from within –
a hunger's seed can reap the harvest.

Accident or purpose no matter
the field you are in has answers.
They will be harder to find in fading light
but we must work with what we have.

Stand by me, there is much to learn
though I am not here to teach
and this is not the start of the journey
for each one of us has a past –
a field set aside is not its full story
of toil and furrow, crops, seasons.

Do not hurry the harvest – the ground
needs prepared – show me your hands
there is work ahead – graft and heft.
Focus, breathe in – use your senses as tools.

I will remain with you a little longer
try to answer your questions.
Still fixated on hedge and fence,
do not take boundaries as a given.
Though this is the far field you can travel on;
beyond those hills lies loch and sea.

Brian Holton

Saumon Lowp

The derk thraw o a bull saumon
Lowpin abune the skinklin watter
Hairst-time sun skimmerin bricht
Aneath the auld brig o rose-reid stane
    At Ettrick Watter's meetin
    Tweed's waters pirlin
    Lapperin awa ti the sea

Frae watter an stane an sun's fire
We cam, a crawl o birselt things
Ti reinge ootowre the turnin yird
Creepin about aa its braw growth
    Oobits happi t wi glory
    Bummin fell roarie
    In the gairden we wir gien

Ablow the soss o the seemin warld
The thrawn thorterie o this an that
It's time at muves our fordovert hairts
Our fordovert hairts at muves in time
    Eagle on the lochan shore
    Bull an saumon, stag an boar
    Ayebydin in the stane

Stewart Sanderson

For W.S. Graham on Ben Narnain

Since all our words are borrowed
just a wee while, from the wind

I send you this – a message
which will never find

you now, so far you've wandered
into that high land

whose only speech is silence
and where all the mountains end.

Yet over the great
Gantries and cantilevers
Of love, a sky, real and
Particular is slowly
Startled into light

'The Dark Dialogues', W.S. Graham

Ian Bamforth

Graham's Landing

'The ear says more
Than any tongue'

I thought I spoke your language
asking what the matter was, the wrong.
I only wanted to know your history
framed in the window of our time.

Which of us should have had first say?
One who inhaled the long firth,
one who seemed a slow-island-Joe,
one who clambered the bare scree up –

The house put on its afternoon disguise,
wrong way round and inside out.
Language was an unreliable hidey-hole
for two social beasts in harness:

me, losing track of the unreliable words
called bait and purchase, you
dangling them in the cold blue sound
that wandered past the window.

Tamar Yoseloff

A Letter to W.S. Graham

Sydney – if I may call you Sydney – because I feel
you have been speaking to me all this time,
in the complex, common tongue you attempted
to decipher. And I've been listening, here
by the sea you said was listening. It is a space,
the sea, like all the other spaces you tried to
(de)construct, it is a poem that finds its turn
along the shoreline; a lament, a plain-
tive voice, like the mother of a drowned child.

The light is variable, and I write to hold it against
the shadows. It's all we can ever do – try to hold
a moment disappearing even as we whisper its name
and place it in the light. Break here, stop
your difficult glances and cantankerous rambles.
Tell me
        how to say something about the sea
that hasn't been said in thousands of words,
stumbling across the page like drunks, none of them
up to the job. The job is love, you said,
that's why we stretch ourselves into a thousand
suffering shapes, like Hilton's nudes or Lanyon's thermals.
You made words of their colours, made words
for the sea that fancies itself a metaphor, too pretty
and brutal for simple truth.
                      Tell me
now that your words are done, how to keep going on.
The coast stretches too far for me to see,
but you're ahead, in a lonely place (we make our own,
you said); from there you must be able to see us all,
lighting lamps with our voices.

Anthony Astbury

Letter to W.S. Graham

I can't say what your letter
means to me – that you 'in bed
hearing the bat and ball
and seeing the gasworks' should
trouble to write saying
good my 'Autobiography'.
I suppose it's because we love
each other. I have you since
reading my first poem 'Gigha'
as a boy. It made a poet
when the words and the sea
came together for me.
I wish I wrote you often
but everything's always been
too much for me to write love much.

Roddy Lumsden

Three Voices

Claim to rope-rein, tow and cladding;
claim to the voices of Leo and Lexy and Jock.
To oversee the child, fuchsia-cheeked all evening.
To oversee the wedding of heights and howes.
To night-walk in the weight of rain
too late for clinch again.
To night-walk in the ambit watch
of beast or brute, a champion of nows.
And Lexy says 'A long night ride into the city'.
And Leo pulls stilts onto his tongue
and talks pan loaf, bool-moued.
And Jock cries claim and acclaim,
his incoming super viewed. And you,
falling evening makes of you
an adjective, a paintable adjective.

The titles are finished
It was a way
Of speaking towards you

'Wynter and the Grammarsow', W.S. Graham

W.S. Graham

[*When I was About Ten in Greenock*]

When I was about ten in Greenock, my mother used to send me away to a distant cooperative at the other end of the town to get tick. It was a great town. Imagine me setting out with my mother's note in my pocket and my basket, running down Hope Street.

Down Hope Street. Along Lyndoch Street halfway. Down Montage Street. I changed my basket because I liked to walk different on every street. Under the big Arch and here I am turning into Mans Lane, the Sugar Works on one side the Bone Works on the other. One side sweet sugar smell with pulleys and belts working. What great workings. I look in the windows covered with dust but there is nobody. Belts whir and I walk with a young joy up between the industries to get out the other side.

This is the town's East End, more exciting for me as a boy. I'm past Scots (where my father used to work on his lathe.) and Clondyke (the old ship-yard.) and Haze's Foundry, the doors open, you could see the furnace.

Anyhow I got to the 'Co' and Minty read my list and filled my basket and gave me a sugar biscuit for going back. I went back another way. I didn't eat my biscuit till Lyndoch Street.

Do you think that was me there as a boy? My mother cuts me a thick slice of bread with apricot jam. My father is coming home at half-past five.

Notes

MONIZA ALVI: 'Motherbird's Bruises'

From the 'Motherbird' series, and inspired by W.S. Graham's 'Enter a Cloud'.

IAIN BAMFORTH: 'Graham's Landing'

'The ear says more / Than any tongue' comes from W.S. Graham's poem 'The Hill of Intrusion' and could stand as a motto for the view of the doctor, patient and illness embraced in the poem 'Doing Calls on the Old Portpatrick Road' of which 'Graham's Landing' is part twelve.

STEPHEN EMMERSON: 'Haunted Water'

The poem was created using lines from W.S. Graham poems. The lines were adapted, and in some cases rewritten, to accommodate the feel of a new poem.

A.B. JACKSON: 'Supper with the Grahams'

Part II is a found or foraged poem, with lines gathered from *Nessie Dunsmuir's Ten Poems* (Greville Press, 1988) – the only poems that she published in her lifetime, written between 1945 and 1949.
In the main, whole lines have been reproduced as they were, with only minor changes to capitalization and punctuation. There are two significant exceptions: line 5 omits the line break of the original 'I would have chosen children, / the breathing hearth', and line 9 is an alternate version of 'Here by the window blackthorn and elder tree'.
The source poems are as follows: 'I Would Have Chosen Children', 'Acorn Mile Miracle Tree', 'To My Father', 'By the Window', 'Stanis Pit', 'The White Word', and 'Raith Pit'.

HUGH MACDIARMID: 'The Royal Stag'

First published in MacDiarmid's *Scottish Eccentrics* in 1936. A copy retitled 'For W.S. Graham' was sent to Graham with a letter (dated 11th April 1970) thanking him for the gift of a copy of *Malcolm Mooney's Land* (Faber and Faber, 1970). The poem bears MacDiarmid's signature, together with the following handwritten dedication: 'For old friendship's sake and in admiration of the way he has always set his 'stout heart to a stey brae' in his undeflected – if still almost unrewarded – devotion to his art of poetry.'

EDWIN MORGAN: '[Verse letter dated 29 October 1950]'

Hospitalised in Truro after a serious leg injury, W.S. Graham was far from home in Zennor. Edwin Morgan lent money to help him cope with the loss of casual earnings. 'Trobar clus' and 'leu' are (respectively) the complex and accessible styles of troubadour poetry. The images of 'golden fell' and 'cinderfall' are from Morgan's poem 'The Sleights of Darkness'. 'The Knight in the Tiger's Skin' is a twelfth-century Georgian epic poem by Shotha Rustaveli.

PETER RILEY: 'A Prelude for W.S.G.'

As well as several subsumed quotations from poems by Graham there is one from Matthew Francis's notes to *New Collected Poems*.

LINDSEY SHIELDS WATERS: 'The Beyst in the Spais'

A translation of W.S. Graham's poem 'The Beast in the Space' into Older Scots.

LAVINIA SINGER: 'A Voice Between Two Things'

The poem incorporates some of Graham's own words, discovered in letters, poems and notebooks while I was undertaking doctoral research.

JOHN WILKINSON: 'Goonhilly Downs'

Goonhilly Downs is the Cornish site of a satellite earth station or 'listening post'.

Contributors and Acknowledgements

Rachael Allen is the poetry editor for *Granta*, co-editor of poetry press Clinic and online journal *Tender*. Her first full collection is forthcoming from Faber and Faber in 2019.

Moniza Alvi was born in Pakistan and grew up in Hertfordshire. Her most recent poetry book *At the Time of Partition* (Bloodaxe Books, 2013) focused on the partition of India and Pakistan and her family history, and was shortlisted for the T.S. Eliot Prize. A new collection *Blackbird, Bye Bye* will appear in 2018. She lives in Norfolk where she tutors for the Poetry School.

Anthony Astbury was born in Bury, Lancashire, in 1940. He served as a ship's writer on the P&O liner SS *Canberra* and taught English and Scripture at a preparatory school in Warwick. He founded The Greville Press in 1975 and has published four collections of verse, edited selections and anthologies, and written memoirs of his friends George Barker, W.S. Graham, John Heath-Stubbs, Harold Pinter and David Wright.

Tim Atkins is the author of many volumes, including *To Repel Ghosts, 1001 Sonnets*, and *Horace*. His *Petrarch Collected Atkins* was a *Times Literary Supplement* Book of the Year for 2014. His most recent collection of poetry is *On Fathers < On Daughtyrs* (Boiler House Press, 2017). A novel, *The Bath-Tub*, is due from Boiler House in 2018.

Iain Bamforth grew up in Glasgow and graduated from its medical school. He has published four collections of poetry, most recently *The Crossing Fee* (Carcanet Press, 2013) and prose publications include *The Body in the Library* (Verso, 2003), *The Good European* (Carcanet Press, 2006) and *A Doctor's Dictionary* (Carcanet Press, 2015). www.iainbamforth.com

Fiona Benson lives in rural Devon with her husband James Meredith and their daughters, Isla and Rose. Her pamphlet was 'Faber New Poets 1' in the Faber New Poets series, and her full-length collection *Bright Travellers* (Jonathan Cape, 2014), received the Seamus Heaney Prize for first collection and the Geoffrey Faber Memorial Prize. Her second book *Vertigo & Ghost* will be published by Cape in 2019.

Paula Bohince is the author of three poetry collections, most recently *Swallows and Waves* (Sarabande, 2016). Her poems have appeared in *The New Yorker, The New York Review of Books, TLS, Granta, The Poetry Review* and elsewhere. She has been a Hawthornden Fellow in Scotland and a reader at the Aldeburgh Poetry Festival. She lives in Pennsylvania, USA.

Andrea Brady's books include *The Strong Room* (Crater, 2016), *Dompteuse* (Bookthug, 2014), *Cut from the Rushes* (Reality Street, 2013), *Mutability: scripts for infancy* (Seagull, 2012), *Wildfire: A Verse Essay on Obscurity and Illumination* (Krupskaya, 2010), and *Vacation of a Lifetime* (Salt, 2001). She is Professor of Poetry at Queen Mary University of London, where she runs the Centre for Poetry and the Archive of the Now (www.archiveofthenow.org). She is co-publisher of Barque Press.

David Briggs is an Eric Gregory Award winner, and appears in the Bloodaxe anthology *Identity Parade: New British and Irish Poets* (2010). He published two full collections with Salt: *The Method Men* (2010), which was shortlisted for the London Festival Poetry Prize, and *Rain Rider* (2013). A chapbook, *Vision Helmet* (2016), is available from Maquette Press. He lives in Bristol.

GEORGE MACKAY BROWN (1921–1996): 'W.S. Graham'. Copyright © the Estate of George Mackay Brown, 1987, 2018. All rights reserved. From *Edinburgh Review*, issue 75, 1987. Reproduced by kind permission of Jenny Brown Associates.

George Mackay Brown was born and lived in Stromness, Orkney, and the character of the Orkney archipelago and its people was central to his work. He was the author of an autobiography, essays, novels, short stories, poetry and plays. His *Collected Poems* were published by Polygon in 2005.

SAM BUCHAN-WATTS: 'Lines Following W.S. Graham's Imagined Forest'. Copyright © Sam Buchan-Watts, 2018. All rights reserved.

Sam Buchan-Watts is co-editor of Clinic Press. His pamphlet was published in 2016 in the Faber New Poets series, and he won an Eric Gregory Award in the same year.

ALAN BUCKLEY: 'Confessional'. Copyright © Alan Buckley, 2018. All rights reserved.

Alan Buckley was brought up on Merseyside. He has had two pamphlets published, *Shiver* (tall-lighthouse, 2009), which was a PBS Pamphlet Choice, and *The Long Haul* (HappenStance, 2016). He was highly commended in the 2017 Forward Prizes. He works in Oxford as a psychotherapist; he is also a poetry editor for ignitionpress, and a school writer in residence with the charity First Story.

JOHN BURNSIDE: 'Fantasia on a Line of W.S. Graham'. Copyright © John Burnside, 2018. All rights reserved.

John Burnside is a novelist, poet and memoirist. His collection *Black Cat Bone* was one of only two poetry collections ever to win both the T.S. Eliot and the Forward Prizes in the same year. He teaches at St Andrews University.

NIALL CAMPBELL: 'Cooling a Meal by the Outside Door'. Copyright © Niall Campbell, 2018. All rights reserved.

Niall Campbell is a poet from the Western Isles of Scotland. His first collection, *Moontide*, was published by Bloodaxe in 2014, and received the Edwin Morgan Poetry Award and Saltire First Book of the Year. He lives in Leeds.

VAHNI CAPILDEO: 'Seastairway'. Copyright © Vahni Capildeo, 2018. All rights reserved.

Vahni Capildeo's most recent books are *Measures of Expatriation* (Carcanet, 2016; Forward Poetry Prize for Best Collection; T.S. Eliot Prize nomination), *Seas and Trees* (IPSI, 2017) and *Venus as a Bear* (Carcanet, 2018). An ex-medievalist, she has worked in lexicography, academia, and culture for development. Current projects include collaborations with Chris McCabe on expanded translation, and with Katy Hastie on image and text. She is a Douglas Caster Cultural Fellow at the University of Leeds.

JIM CARRUTH: 'Far Field 3'. Copyright © Jim Carruth, 2018. All rights reserved.

Jim Carruth is the Glasgow Poet Laureate. His first collection, *Killochries*, was shortlisted for the Saltire Scottish Poetry Book of the Year, the Seamus Heaney Centre for Poetry Prize and the Fenton Aldeburgh Prize for first collection. He is founder and current chair of St Mungo's Mirrorball – the Glasgow poetry network – and artistic adviser for StAnza poetry festival. His most recent collection, *Black Cart*, was published in 2017.

CHARLES CAUSLEY (1917–2003): 'Letter to W.S. Graham'. Copyright © the Estate of Charles Causley, 2000, 2018. All rights reserved. From *Collected Poems (1951–2000)* (Picador, 2000). Reproduced by kind permission of David Higham Associates.

Charles Causley (CBE, FRSL) was born and lived in Launceston, Cornwall. He served in the Royal Navy during the Second World War and worked as a primary school teacher. He wrote for children and adults, and was awarded the Queen's Gold Medal for Poetry in 1967. His *Collected Poems (1951–2000)* are published by Picador.

JOHN WEDGWOOD CLARKE: 'Peter Lanyon'. Copyright © John Wedgwood Clarke, 2018. All rights reserved.

John Wedgwood Clarke was born and raised in St Ives, Cornwall. He is a lecturer in creative writing at the University of Exeter and has published two full collections of poems, *Ghost Pot* (2013) and *Landfill* (2017), both with Valley Press.

KELVIN CORCORAN: 'Forty-five Lines on W.S. Graham'. Copyright © Kelvin Corcoran, 2018. All rights reserved.

Kelvin Corcoran lives in Brussels. He is the author of sixteen books of poetry including, most recently, *Facing West*, 2017, and the Medicine Unboxed commissioned *Not Much To Say Really*, 2017. The sequence 'Helen Mania' was a Poetry Book Society Choice and the poem 'At the Hospital Doors' was highly commended by the Forward Prize 2017. His work is the subject of a study edited by Professor Andy Brown, *The Poetry Occurs as Song*, 2013.

ROBERT CRAWFORD: 'Port'. Copyright © Robert Crawford, 2016, 2018. All rights reserved. The poem first appeared in *Archipelago* (Issue 11, Winter 2016).

Robert Crawford's seventh collection of poems, *Testament*, was published by Cape in 2014. He is an award-winning biographer, critic and Bishop Wardlaw Professor of Poetry at the University of St Andrews. His next collection, *The Scottish Ambassador*, will be published in August 2018.

EMILY CRITCHLEY: 'In Memory W.S. Graham'. Copyright © Emily Critchley, 2018. All rights reserved.

Emily Critchley most recent collection is *Ten Thousand Things* (Boiler House Press, 2017). She has published critical articles on poetry, philosophy and feminism, and is the editor of *Out of Everywhere 2: Linguistically Innovative Poetry by Women in North America & the UK* (Reality Street, 2016). Critchley is Senior Lecturer in English and Creative Writing at the University of Greenwich, London.

TIM CUMMING: 'The Sound'. Copyright © Tim Cumming, 2018. All rights reserved.

Tim Cumming's first collection, *The Miniature Estate*, was published in 1991, and subsequent books include *Apocalypso* (1992, 1999, 2004), *Contact Print* (2002), *The Rumour* (2004), *The Rapture* (2011), *Etruscan Miniatures* (2012) and *Rebel Angels in the Mind Shop* (2015). His film poems have been screened internationally and he has exhibited poems and paintings at Sladers Yard gallery in Dorset. He lives and works in London.

SASHA DUGDALE: 'Headland'. Copyright © Sasha Dugdale, 2018. All rights reserved.

Sasha Dugdale has published four collections of poetry, the most recent of which, *Joy*, (Carcanet Press, 2017) was PBS Winter Choice. The collection is named after her long poem 'Joy' which won the Forward Prize for Best Single Poem. She translates poetry and plays from Russian and has worked with theatres across the UK and US on productions of contemporary Russian plays. She is currently working on translations of Maria Stepanova's poems for UK publication. Sasha was editor of *Modern Poetry in Translation* and co-editor of the anthology *Centres of Cataclysm* (Bloodaxe, 2016).

IAN DUHIG: 'Glass Words'. Copyright Ian Duhig, 2018. All rights reserved.

Ian Duhig has written seven books of poetry, most recently *The Blind Roadmaker* (Picador, 2016), a Poetry Book Society Recommendation shortlisted for the Roehampton, T.S. Eliot and Forward Prizes. In 2017 he contributed to *Refugee Tales II* and is currently working on his *Selected Poems*.

RONNIE DUNCAN: 'For W.S. Graham'. Copyright © Ronnie Duncan, 1987, 2018. All rights reserved.

Ronnie Duncan is a former businessman and a life-long collector of contemporary art. His first love, however, was poetry. He had a twenty-seven-year correspondence with W.S. Graham and made tape recordings of the author. He also organised a W.S. Graham celebration for the Ilkley Literature Festival in 1994. A film (*More Luck Than Money*) about his house and stone garden can be found online.

DOUGLAS DUNN: '"One Renfrewshire Man to Another"'. Copyright © Douglas Dunn, 2018. All rights reserved.

Douglas Dunn was born in Inchinnan, Renfrewshire in 1942, and was Professor in the School of English at the University of St Andrews. As well as over ten collections of poetry, he has written radio and television plays and edited anthologies. He was awarded an OBE in 2003 and the Queen's Gold Medal for Poetry in 2013. His most recent collection is *The Noise of a Fly* (Faber and Faber, 2017).

NESSIE DUNSMUIR (1909–1999): 'For a Winter Lover'. Copyright © the Estate of Nessie Dunsmuir, 1988, 2018. All rights reserved. From *Nessie Dunsmuir's Ten Poems* (The Greville Press, 1988). Reproduced by kind permission of Rosalind Mudaliar, the Estate of Nessie Dunsmuir.

Nessie Dunsmuir was born in Blantyre, Scotland. She met W.S. Graham at the Workers' Education Association college at Newbattle Abbey, near Edinburgh, and they married in 1954. A pamphlet of her poetry, *Nessie Dunsmuir's Ten Poems* was published by The Greville Press in 1988.

STEPHEN EMMERSON: 'Haunted Water'. Copyright © Stephen Emmerson, 2018. All rights reserved.

Stephen Emmerson is the author of: *Telegraphic Transcriptions, Family Portraits, Poetry Wholes, & The Journal of Baal*. He also makes poetry objects. More info here https://stephenemmerson.wordpress.com

CARRIE ETTER: 'One for London'. Copyright © Carrie Etter, 2018. All rights reserved.

Carrie Etter's third and most recent collection, *Imagined Sons* (Seren, 2014), was shortlisted for the Ted Hughes Award for New Work in Poetry, and her fourth, *The Weather in Normal*, will appear late in 2018. She is Reader in Creative Writing at Bath Spa University.

MATTHEW FRANCIS: 'A Dream of Cornwall'. Copyright © Matthew Francis, 2018. All rights reserved.

Matthew Francis is the author of five Faber collections, most recently his poetic version of *The Mabinogi*. In 2004 he was chosen as one of the Next Generation Poets. He has edited W. S. Graham's *New Collected Poems* and published a collection of short stories and two novels, the second of which, *The Book of the Needle*, came out in 2014. He lives in west Wales and is Professor of Creative Writing at Aberystwyth University.

ANNIE FREUD: 'Sydney on the Street of Knives'. Copyright © Annie Freud, 2018. All rights reserved.

Annie Freud is a poet, teacher and artist. Her first collection *The Best Man That Ever Was* (Picador, 2007) received a Poetry Book Society recommendation and was awarded the Dimplex Prize for New Writing. *The Mirabelles* (Picador, 2010) was a Poetry Book Society Choice and shortlisted for the T.S. Eliot Prize. Her third collection *The Remains* (Picador, 2015) was awarded a Poetry Book Society Recommendation. Annie was named by the Poetry Book Society as one of the Next Generation Poets (2014).

DAI GEORGE: 'The Continual Other Offer'. Copyright © Dai George, 2018. All rights reserved.

Dai George's first collection was *The Claims Office* (Seren, 2013), an *Evening Standard* book of the year. He is an editor at the online journal *Prac Crit* and a PhD student at University College London.

ALAN GILLIS: 'The Interior'. Copyright © Alan Gillis, 2018. All rights reserved.

Alan Gillis is from Belfast and teaches English Literature at the University of Edinburgh. His poetry collection *Scapegoat* (2014) followed *Here Comes the Night* (2010), *Hawks and Doves* (2007) and *Somebody, Somewhere* (2004), all published by Gallery Press. He was chosen by the Poetry Book Society as a Next Generation Poet in 2014.

PETER GIZZI: 'A Round for W.S. Graham'. Copyright © Peter Gizzi, 2018. All rights reserved.

Peter Gizzi is the author of seven collections of poetry, most recently, *Archeophonics* (finalist for the National Book Award), *In Defense of Nothing: Selected Poems 1987–2011* and *Threshold Songs*. His honours include the Lavan Younger Poet Award from the Academy of American Poets, and fellowships in poetry from The Rex Foundation, The Howard Foundation, The Foundation for Contemporary Arts, The John Simon Guggenheim Memorial Foundation and The Judith E. Wilson Visiting Fellowship in Poetry at the University of Cambridge. He works at the University of Massachusetts, Amherst, USA.

JANE GOLDMAN: 'Everything SOLID'. Copyright © Jane Goldman, 2018. All rights reserved.

Jane Goldman lives in Edinburgh and is Reader in English at Glasgow University. Her poems have been published in *Gutter*, *Blackbox Manifold*, *Tender*, *Front Horse*, *Adjacent Pineapple* and elsewhere. Her first slim volume is *Border Thoughts* (Leamington Books, 2014), 'a little theatrical box of spectacle and light […] the living underworld of Brecht's Threepenny Opera translated into raucous girlish post-war wayward ways' (*Hix Eros*).

W.S. GRAHAM: '[And Who Will Hold Me in the Dark]', 'An Entertainment for W.S. Graham for Him Having Reached Sixty-five', '[As the Tide was Streaming Out]', 'Evening on Loch Long', 'For Robert Brennan', '[It is as Though the Very Movement Comes Out of Silence]', '[Late Between Disguises]', '[Less Than the Edge of a Rain Flute]', 'Lines for a Poster', 'Lost Somewhere Between Krista and Nicolaos', 'Or from Your Emerald Office are You Able', 'The Answerers', '[The Boundaries]', 'The Contemporary Dear', 'The Curlew', 'The Owl', '[Thirty-six Implements]', '[To Sheila Lanyon, on the Flyleaf of a Book]', '[What We Call the World]', '[When I was About Ten in Greenock]'. Copyright © the Estate of W.S. Graham, 2018. All rights reserved. Published by kind permission of Rosalind Mudaliar, the Estate of W.S. Graham.

KATHRYN GRAY: 'Difficult Ones'. Copyright © Kathryn Gray, 2018. All rights reserved.

Kathryn Gray's *The Never-Never* (Seren, 2004) was shortlisted for the T. S. Eliot Prize and the Forward Prize for Best First Collection. Her latest publication is a pamphlet, *Flowers*, from Rack Press.

VONA GROARKE: 'The Choosing'. Copyright © Vona Groarke, 2018. All rights reserved.

Vona Groarke has published seven collections of poetry with Gallery Press, most recently X (2014) and *Selected Poems*, awarded the Pigott Prize for the best Irish book of poetry in 2016. Her book-length essay on art frames, *Four Sides Full*, was also published in 2016. Her poems have recently appeared in *The New Yorker*, *Ploughshares* and *Threepenny Review*. Former editor of *Poetry Ireland Review*, she is a Senior Lecturer in poetry at the University of Manchester.

JEN HADFIELD: 'The Porcelain Cliff'. Copyright © Jen Hadfield, 2018. All rights reserved.

Jen Hadfield was born in Cheshire and home is Shetland, whose landscape and natural life persistently informs her work. Her second poetry book *Nigh-No-Place* (Bloodaxe Books, 2008) won the T.S. Eliot Prize. Her third, *Byssus*, was published by Picador in 2014. In 2016–17, she was the Writer in Residence for Glasgow University and the Glasgow School of Art, supported by Creative Scotland. @hadfield_jen | www.panmacmillan.com/authors/jen-hadfield

ALAN HALSEY: 'Dear WSG'. Copyright © Alan Halsey, 2018. All rights reserved.

Alan Halsey's *Selected Poems 1988–2016* is published by Shearsman. His other books include *The Text of Shelley's Death*, *Marginalien & Lives of the Poets* (all from Five Seasons) and *Versions of Martial* (Knives Forks & Spoons). He is an affiliated poet at Sheffield University's Centre for Poetry & Poetics.

LESLEY HARRISON: 'Ilulissat'. Copyright © Lesley Harrison, 2018. All rights reserved. From *Blue Pearl* (New Directions, 2017). Reproduced by kind permission of the author.

Lesley Harrison lives on the Angus coast of Scotland. In her poetry and prose she explores our instinctive responses to landscape – physical, material, linguistic, psychological. Recent projects include working with scientists and visual artists to produce a multimedia 'deep map' of the Icelandic fishing village Skagaströnd. Her most recent pamphlet is *Blue Pearl* (New Directions, 2017).

PAUL HENRY: 'Violin Tide'. Copyright © Paul Henry, 2010, 2018. All rights reserved. From *The Brittle Sea: New & Selected Poems* (Seren Books, 2010). Reproduced by kind permission of Seren Books.

Paul Henry came to poetry through songwriting. His publications include *The Brittle Sea: New & Selected Poems*, *Boy Running* and *The Glass Aisle*. A Writing Fellow at the University of South Wales, he wrote and presented *Do Not Expect Applause: the Life and Work of W.S. Graham* for BBC Radio 3. paulhenrywales.co.uk @theglassaisle

W.N. HERBERT: 'The Nightfishing'. Copyright © W.N. Herbert, 2018. All rights reserved.

W.N. Herbert was born in Dundee in 1961 and lives in Newcastle, where he is Professor of Poetry and Creative Writing at Newcastle University. He is mostly published by Bloodaxe Books; recent publications include *Omnesia* and, with Donut Press, *Murder Bear*. He is a Fellow of the Royal Society of Literature and also the Dundee Makar.

BRIAN HOLTON: 'Saumon Lowp'. Copyright © Brian Holton, 2018. All rights reserved.

Brian Holton was born in Galashiels and taught Chinese language and literature and translation. He has translated a dozen books by the contemporary poet Yang Lian, and *Staunin Ma Lane*, a collection of classical Chinese poetry in Scots. He won first prize for Scots in the inaugural Tannahill Poetry Competition. He has travelled widely in the Far East, and lives in Melrose with an unfeasibly large number of musical instruments and a bicycle.

SARAH HOWE: 'Waking'. Copyright © Sarah Howe, 2018. All rights reserved.

Sarah Howe is a Hong Kong-born poet, academic and editor. Her first book, *Loop of Jade*, (Chatto & Windus, 2015) won the T.S. Eliot Prize. She is the founding editor of *Prac Crit*, an online journal of poetry and criticism, and teaches poetry at King's College London.

ALEXANDER HUTCHISON (1943–2015): 'Setting the Time Aside'. Copyright © the Estate of Alexander Hutchison, 2013, 2018. All rights reserved. From *Bones & Breath* (Salt Publishing, 2013). Reproduced by kind permission of the Estate of Alexander Hutchison.

Alexander Hutchison was born in Buckie, Scotland. His first collection, *Deep-tap Tree*, was published in the USA in 1978, and his last, *Gavia Stellata* – a selection of poems in English and Spanish translation (by Juana Adcock) – in Mexico, shortly before his death. His collection *Bones & Breath* (Salt Publishing, 2013) was awarded the Saltire Award for Best Poetry Book of the Year in 2014.

A.B. JACKSON: 'Supper with the Grahams'. Copyright © A.B. Jackson, 2018. All rights reserved.

A.B. Jackson was born in Glasgow and spent his childhoods in Cheshire and Fife before studying English Literature at the University of Edinburgh. His first book, *Fire Stations*, won the Forward Prize for Best First Collection in 2003. His latest collection, *The Wilderness Party* (Bloodaxe Books, 2015), is a Poetry Book Society Recommendation. He is currently working on a third full-length collection, *The Voyage of St Brendan*.

JACKIE KAY: 'Out of the Clyde'. Copyright © Jackie Kay, 2018. All rights reserved.

Jackie Kay was born and brought up in Scotland. Her work has won numerous awards, including the Forward Prize, Saltire Prize, the Scottish Arts Council Prize and the Guardian Fiction Award. She has received an MBE and is fellow to the Royal Society of Literature. She is Chancellor of the University of Salford and Professor of Creative Writing at Newcastle University. Jackie was named Scots Makar – the National Poet for Scotland – in March 2016.

LINDA KEMP: 'Silent Coast'. Copyright © Linda Kemp, 2018. All rights reserved.

Linda Kemp's poetry publications include *Lease Prise Redux* (Materials, 2016) and an album, *speaking towards* (2015). Linda is editor at Enjoy Your Homes Press.

AMY KEY: 'How Do You Feel About Me Being Gone Forever?' Copyright © Amy Key, 2018. All rights reserved.

Amy Key's first collection *Luxe* was published by Salt in 2013. She is the author of two pamphlets, *Instead of Stars* (Tall Lighthouse) and *History* (If A Leaf Falls Press). Her second book-length collection, *Isn't Forever*, is due from Bloodaxe in June 2018.

L.M. KILBRIDE: 'I Plant the Seed Within Myself', Copyright © L.M. Kilbride, 2018. All rights reserved.

L.M. Kilbride grew up in York and studied at Cambridge, where she was introduced to Graham's work by the poet Ian Patterson. Her poetry publications include *Errata* and *In the Square*. She is presently at work on a new collection of shorter poems called *Volta*.

ZAFFAR KUNIAL: 'W*nd'. Copyright © Zaffar Kunial, 2018. All rights reserved.

Zaffar Kunial was born in Birmingham and lives in Hebden Bridge. His pamphlet *Faber New Poets 11* was published in 2014. An essay 'Laburnum Time' was collected in the anthology of woodland writing, *Arboreal* (Little Toller, 2016). His first full poetry collection is due with Faber & Faber in 2018.

DAVID KINLOCH: 'A Vision of W.S. Graham's Hippopotamus in Venice'. Copyright © David Kinloch, 2001, 2018. All right reserved. From *Un Tour d'Ecosse* (Carcanet Press, 2001). Reproduced by kind permission of Carcanet Press.

David Kinloch was born in Glasgow and has published six collections of poetry. He teaches creative writing and Scottish literature at the University of Strathclyde, Glasgow. He was a founder editor of the poetry magazine *Verse* and in 2004 he was a winner of the Robert Louis Stevenson Memorial Award. His latest collection is *In Search of Dustie-Fute* (Carcanet Press, 2017).

PIPPA LITTLE: 'Not Earthed but Longing'. Copyright © Pippa Little, 2018. All rights reserved.

Pippa Little is a Royal Literary Fund fellow at Newcastle University. Her second full collection, *Twist*, was published by Arc in 2017 and shortlisted for The Saltire Society's Best Poetry Book Award.

TONY LOPEZ: 'Go Back'. Copyright © Tony Lopez, 2018. All rights reserved.

Tony Lopez has been to Greenock and to Madron and to Malcolm Mooney's Land; he almost didn't come back. He wrote *The Poetry of W.S. Graham* (Edinburgh University Press, 1989) a very long time ago. His poetry books include *False Memory*; a second edition of which is available from Shearsman.

HANNAH LOWE: 'River'. Copyright © Hannah Lowe, 2018. All rights reserved.

Hannah Lowe's first poetry collection *Chick* (Bloodaxe, 2013) won the Michael Murphy Memorial Award for Best First Collection. In September 2014, she was named as one of twenty Next Generation Poets. Her second collection, *Chan*, is published by Bloodaxe. (2016). She lectures at Brunel University and is the current Poet in Residence at Keats House.

RODDY LUMSDEN: 'Three Voices'. Copyright Roddy Lumsden, 2018. All rights reserved.

Roddy Lumsden was born in St Andrews and is the author of ten collections of poetry; the most recent, *So Glad I'm Me* (Bloodaxe Books, 2017) was shortlisted for the T.S. Eliot Prize. He edited the anthology *Identity Parade: New British and Irish Poets* (Bloodaxe Books, 2010), co-edited *The Salt Book of Younger Poets* (Salt Publishing, 2011) and has represented Scotland in BBC Radio 4's *Round Britain Quiz*.

HUGH MACDIARMID (1892–1978): 'The Royal Stag'. Copyright © the Estate of Hugh MacDiarmid, 1936, 2017, 2018. All rights reserved. From *Complete Poems, Volume One* (Carcanet Press, 2017). Reproduced by kind permission of Carcanet Press.

Hugh MacDiarmid is the pen name of Christopher Murray Grieve. He was born in Langholm, Scotland, and was a poet, journalist, essayist and political figure who championed Scottish nationalism and was the principal force behind the Scottish Literary Renaissance of the early- to mid-twentieth century. He wrote in Scots and English.

PETER MANSON: 'To Peter Manson'. Copyright © Peter Manson, 2018. All rights reserved.

Peter Manson lives in Glasgow. His books include *Adjunct: an Undigest, Between Cup and Lip, English in Mallarmé, For the Good of Liars* and *Poems of Frank Rupture*. His book of translations, *Stéphane Mallarmé: The Poems in Verse* is published by Miami University Press, Ohio. His website is petermanson.wordpress.com

MARION MCCREADY: 'Night Crossing'. Copyright © Marion McCready, 2017, 2018. All rights reserved. From *Madame Ecosse* (Eyewear Publishing, 2017). Reproduced by kind permission of Eyewear Publishing.

Marion McCready lives in Dunoon, Argyll. She won a Scottish Book Trust New Writers Award, and the Melita Hume Poetry Prize for her first full-length poetry collection *Tree Language* which was published by Eyewear Publishing in 2014. Her second collection *Madame Ecosse* was published in 2017, also by Eyewear.

ANDREW MCNEILLIE: 'Night-Snow'. Copyright © Andrew McNeillie, 2010, 2018. All rights reserved. From *In Mortal Memory* (Carcanet Press, 2010). Reproduced by kind permission of Carcanet Press.

Andrew McNeillie was born in North Wales. He held a chair in English at Exeter University where he is now Emeritus Professor. He is the founding editor of the magazine *Archipelago* and runs Clutag Press. His most recent collection is *Winter Moorings* (Carcanet Press, 2014).

EDWIN MORGAN (1920–2010): '[Verse letter dated 29 October 1950]'. Copyright © the Estate of Edwin Morgan, 2015, 2018. From *The Midnight Letterbox*, edited by John Coyle and James McGonigal (Carcanet Press, 2015). Reproduced by kind permission of Carcanet Press.

Edwin Morgan was born and lived in Glasgow. He became lecturer in English at the University of Glasgow, from which he retired as Professor in 1980. He was appointed Poet Laureate of Glasgow in 1999, and received the Queen's Gold Medal for Poetry in 2000. He was appointed Scotland's first Makar, or Poet Laureate, in 2004.

RICHARD PRICE: 'Are You Still There?' Copyright © Richard Price, 2018. All rights reserved.

Richard Price is a writer whose work combines an exploratory imagination with a strong sense of the play, social intensities, and responsibilities of language. His collection *Lucky Day* was shortlisted for the Whitbread Poetry Prize, while *Small World* won the SMIT Poetry Book of the Year Award. Other collections include *Greenfields*, *Rays*, and *Moon for Sale* (all Carcanet Press). He grew up in Renfrewshire, Scotland, and is Head of Contemporary British Collections at the British Library, London.

MEL PRYOR: 'In a Secondhand Bookshop'. Copyright © Mel Pryor, 2018. All rights reserved.

Mel Pryor has won the Essex Poetry Prize, the Ware Sonnet Prize and the Philip Larkin Poetry Prize. She has published a pamphlet, *Drawn on Water* (Eyewear, 2014), and a full collection, *Small Nuclear Family* (Eyewear, 2015). *Small Nuclear Family* was chosen by Bel Mooney as a Christmas choice in the *Daily Mail* and the *TLS* described it as 'a remarkable debut.'

DENISE RILEY: 'Three Awkward Ears'. Copyright © Denise Riley, 2018. All rights reserved.

Denise Riley's books include *War in the Nursery* (1983); *'Am I that Name?'* (1988); *The Words of Selves* (2000); *Denise Riley: Selected Poems* (2000); *The Force of Language*, with Jean-Jacques Lecercle (2004); *Impersonal Passion* (2005); *Time Lived, Without Its Flow* (2012) and *Say Something Back* (2016). She lives in London.

PETER RILEY: 'A Prelude for W.S.G.'. Copyright © Peter Riley, 2018. All rights reserved.

Peter Riley was born in Stockport in 1940 and recently retired to Hebden Bridge after living for twenty-eight years in Cambridge. He is the author of fifteen books of poetry, most recently *Due North* (Shearsman, 2015) which was shortlisted for the Forward Prize for Best Collection, and two pamphlets issued by Calder Valley Poetry, *Pennine Tales* (2016) and *Hushings* (2017).

STEWART SANDERSON: 'To W.S. Graham on Ben Narnain'. Copyright © Stewart Sanderson, 2018. All rights reserved.

Stewart Sanderson is a poet from Glasgow. Twice shortlisted for the Edwin Morgan Poetry Award (2014; 2016), in 2015 he received an Eric Gregory Award for his debut pamphlet, *Fios*, published that year by Aberdeenshire press Tapsalteerie. In 2016 he was awarded a Robert Louis Stevenson Fellowship. He is currently working on a first full-length collection of poems.

LINDSEY SHIELDS WATERS: 'The Beyst in the Spais'. Copyright © Lindsey Shields Waters, 2018. All rights reserved.

Lindsey Shields Waters works as a solicitor at the University of Strathclyde and lives in Glasgow with her family. She completed an MLitt in Creative Writing at the University of Glasgow (with distinction) in 2016 and was a Clydebuilt mentee for 2016–17. She has lived and worked in Washington DC, Bavaria and Leiden, and her poems have been published in *Lighthouse Literary Journal* (Issues 12 and 14) and *Magma Poetry* (Issue 69).

PENELOPE SHUTTLE: 'Mac Lir'. Copyright © Penelope Shuttle, 2018. All rights reserved.

Penelope Shuttle lives in Cornwall. Her twelfth collection, *Will You Walk a Little Faster?* appeared from Bloodaxe Books in May 2017, and was Poetry Book of the Month in *The Observer*. Her next publication is *Lzrd*, (in collaboration with Alyson Hallett), poems about The Lizard Peninsula, Indigo Dreams Publications, Spring 2018.

LAVINIA SINGER: 'A Voice Between Two Things'. Copyright © Lavinia Singer, 2018. All rights reserved.

Lavinia Singer lives in London. Her poetry explores image-making and materiality, and has appeared in various magazines, journals and anthologies. She works as the poetry editorial assistant at Faber and Faber.

MATTHEW SWEENEY: 'Sausages'. Copyright © Matthew Sweeney, 2013, 2018. All rights reserved. From *Horse Music* (Bloodaxe Books, 2013). Reproduced by kind permission of Bloodaxe Books.

Matthew Sweeney's most recent collection, *Inquisition Lane*, came out from Bloodaxe in 2015. Previous collection, *Horse Music* (Bloodaxe Books, 2013) won the inaugural Piggott Poetry Prize. A new book, *My Life as a Painter*, is forthcoming from Bloodaxe in 2018, and a book of prose poems, *King of a Rainy Country*, from Arc.

HELEN TOOKEY: 'Boat'. Copyright © Helen Tookey, 2018. All rights reserved.

Helen Tookey's debut *Missel-Child* (Carcanet, 2014) was shortlisted for the Seamus Heaney prize. Her pamphlet *In the Glasshouse* was published by HappenStance Press in 2016, and she is working on a second full collection. She collaborated with singer/songwriter Sharron Kraus on the CD/booklet *If You Put Out Your Hand* (Wounded Wolf Press, 2016), and is currently collaborating with sound artist/composer Martin Heslop.

KATHARINE TOWERS: 'The Good Words'. Copyright © Katharine Towers, 2018. All rights reserved.

Katharine Towers has published two poetry collections, both with Picador. *The Floating Man* (2010) won the Seamus Heaney Centre Prize and *The Remedies* (2016) was shortlisted for the T.S. Eliot Prize. Her poems have appeared in *The Poetry Review*, *The Guardian* and *Poetry London*. She lives in the Peak District and works as an editor at Candlestick Press.

TIM TURNBULL: 'Meanwhile, None of This is Happening'. Copyright © Tim Turnbull, 2018. All rights reserved.

Tim Turnbull's poetry collections, *Stranded in Sub-Atomica* (2005), *Caligula on Ice and Other Poems* (2009), are published by Donut Press. *Stranded* was shortlisted for the Forward Prize for Best First Collection. He was awarded the Arts Foundation Fellowship for Performance Poetry in 2006. A third collection, *Avanti!*, is due from Red Squirrel Press. In a previous life he worked in forestry. More recently he has been involved in adult literacy work, mostly in prisons.

AHREN WARNER: "Into that almost glade". Copyright © Ahren Warner, 2017, 2018. All Rights reserved. From *Hello. Your promise has been extracted* (Bloodaxe Books, 2017). Reproduced by kind permission of Bloodaxe Books.

Ahren Warner's first collection, *Confer* (Bloodaxe Books, 2011), was shortlisted for the Forward Prize for Best First Collection and the Michael Murphy Memorial Prize 2013. He was awarded an Arts Foundation Fellowship in 2012. His second collection, *Pretty* (2013), and his third, *Hello. Your promise has been extracted* (2017) received Poetry Book Society Recommendations. He is Poetry Editor of *Poetry London*.

NUALA WATT: 'Dear Words'. Copyright © Nuala Watt, 2018. All rights reserved.

Nuala Watt lives in Glasgow. She has a PhD from the University of Glasgow on the poetics of partial sight, dependency and open form. Poems have appeared in *Gutter*, *The Scotsman*, *Wordgathering* and on BBC Radio 3. A pamphlet, *Dialogue on the Dark* came out with Calderwood Press in 2015. Her work features in *Stairs and Whispers: D/deaf and Disabled Poets Write Back* (Nine Arches Press, 2017).

MATTHEW WELTON: 'Which of us is it I am?'. Copyright © Matthew Welton, 2018. All rights reserved.

Matthew Welton was born in 1969 in Nottingham, where he lives and teaches at the University. Much of his writing centres on taking a playful approach to language. He has published three books of poems with Carcanet, and, more recently, the pamphlets *Squid Squad* (Moschatel) and *Five pieces, each of 250 words* (if a leaf falls press).

DAVID WHEATLEY: 'Roger Hilton, *November '64*'. Copyright © David Wheatley, 2018. All rights reserved.

David Wheatley is the author of several volumes of poetry, including *The President of Planet Earth* (Carcanet, 2017). He has also written a critical study, *Contemporary British Poetry* (Palgrave, 2015) and edited the poetry of Samuel Beckett for Faber and Faber. He lives with his wife and son in rural Aberdeenshire.

JOHN WILKINSON: 'On Goonhilly Downs'. Copyright © John Wilkinson, 2018. All rights reserved.

John Wilkinson is a poet and a professor at the University of Chicago who has written about W.S. Graham. He grew up on the Cornish coast and on Dartmoor. *Schedule of Unrest*, his selected poems, was published in 2014 by Salt, and a further collection, *Ghost Nets*, was published in 2016 by Omnidawn.

TONY WILLIAMS: 'Reading WSG at Loch Earn'. Copyright © Tony Williams, 2018. All rights reserved.

Tony Williams's poetry publications include *The Midlands* and *The Corner of Arundel Lane and Charles Street*, which was shortlisted for the Aldeburgh, Portico and Michael Murphy Prizes. His outsider art sonnet sequence, *All the Rooms of Uncle's Head*, was a PBS Pamphlet Choice. He lives in rural Northumberland.

TAMAR YOSELOFF: 'A Letter to W.S. Graham'. Copyright © Tamar Yoseloff, 2015, 2018. All rights reserved. From *A Formula for Night: New and Selected Poems* (Seren Books, 2015). Reproduced by kind permission of Seren Books.

Tamar Yoseloff's fifth collection, *A Formula for Night: New and Selected Poems*, was published by Seren in 2015. She is also the author of *Formerly*, a chapbook incorporating photographs by Vici MacDonald (Hercules Editions, 2012) shortlisted for the Ted Hughes Award. She is currently a visiting guest lecturer at Newcastle University on the Newcastle / Poetry School MA.

Source notes for poems by W.S. Graham

'[And Who Will Hold Me in the Dark]': An undated manuscript fair copy. From the green workbook (1973–1974), W.S. Graham Estate archive.

'An Entertainment for W.S. Graham for Him Having Reached Sixty-five': An undated manuscript draft, with corrections. Possibly written during the summer of 1983, prior to Graham's sixty-fifth birthday on November 19th. W.S. Graham Estate archive.

'[As the Tide was Streaming Out]': This poem is a composite of two drafts; one lengthy, dated 6th May 1966, held at the National Library of Scotland, Edinburgh [Acc. 26019] and the second, a single (first) stanza, from a notebook given to Bryan Wynter, also held at the NLS [Acc. 12979]. Graham also includes this alternative version of the first stanza in a letter to Tony O'Malley, dated 20th August 1969: see pages 228–9 in *The Nightfisherman* (Carcanet Press, 1999). In stanza five, Graham's original line six read 'Between the shadows'. A manuscript note, however, offers 'morning' as a potential alternative for 'shadows'; the editors felt that 'morning' was the stronger of the two options.

'Evening on Loch Long': Undated typescript fair copy. The poem was intended to be the first section of an unfinished poem titled 'Pictures Speaking with Words'. W.S. Graham Estate archive.

'For Robert Brennan': Typescript fair copy. Title and date (27th July 1966) added in the author's hand, together with the message 'Robert, sorry we missed you. Love WSG.' Held by the Estate of Robert Brennan.

'[It is as Though the Very Movement Comes Out of Silence]': An undated typescript fair copy. W.S. Graham Estate archive.

'[Late Between Disguises]': A typescript fragment, with manuscript corrections. Dated in the author's handwriting, 5th May 1973. From the green workbook (1973–1974), W.S. Graham Estate archive.

'[Less Than the Edge of a Rain Flute]': An undated typescript draft with a single manuscript correction. The 'Gitings' appears to be a neologism which refers to the villages Temple Guiting, Guiting Power and the surrounding area to the east of Cleeve Hill and the Cheltenham racecourse in Gloucestershire. From the green workbook (1973–1974), W.S. Graham Estate archive.

'Lines for a Poster': Typescript draft, dated 1968. Robin Skelton Special Collection, University of Victoria, British Columbia, Canada.

'Lost Somewhere Between Krista and Nicolaos': An undated typescript draft with manuscript corrections. W.S. Graham Estate archive.

'Or from Your Emerald Office are You Able': An undated typescript draft, with a single manuscript correction. W.S. Graham Estate archive.

'The Answerers': A typescript draft with manuscript corrections, dated 9th December 1975. The author did not employ capitalisation or italics in the phrase 'the fighting temeraire', to indicate a reference to either the ship (HMS *Temeraire*) or J.M.W. Turner's famous painting of it (*The Fighting Temeraire*). As his intention has been impossible for the editors to ascertain, a decision was made to leave the phrase unchanged. From the green workbook (1973–1974), W.S. Graham Estate archive.

'[The Boundaries]': A typescript draft dated 15th February 1976. The draft indicates that these four stanzas were to be part two of a poem, though no further related drafts have been found. From the green workbook (1973–1974), W.S. Graham Estate Archive.

'The Contemporary Dear': A typescript fair copy, dated in the author's hand 5th May 1960. From Acc.26019 at the National Library of Scotland.

'The Curlew': An undated typescript with a single manuscript correction. From a folder titled *25 Birds*. This project, possibly a commission, was not completed. W.S. Graham Estate archive.

'The Owl': An undated typescript draft with a single manuscript correction. From a folder titled *25 Birds*. W.S. Graham Estate archive.

'[Thirty-six Implements]': The implements included are drawn from three sources: the W.S. Graham Estate archive, the Robin Skelton Special Collection, University of Victoria, British Columbia, Canada, and [Acc.13815] the National Library of Scotland. In the implement beginning 'Ben Narnain was a love of mine,' the editors felt W.S. Graham's misspelling of Soor Duik ('Soordook') was intentional, so have left it uncorrected. Likewise, in the implement beginning 'Illmannered Muse, or maybe only' the editors have chosen not to hyphenate 'Illmannered'.

'[To Sheila Lanyon, on the Flyleaf of a Book]': Inscribed by the author on the flyleaf of a copy of his book *The White Threshold* (Faber and Faber, 1949) belonging to Sheila Lanyon, widow of the painter Peter Lanyon. The 'Second Summer' referred to is the second since Peter's death on 31st August 1964. The poem also exists as a typescript fair copy given to Sheila Lanyon. Both are dated 18th June 1966. From the Peter Lanyon family archive.

'[What We Call the World]': Typescript draft, dated 1972. Robin Skelton Special Collection, University of Victoria, British Columbia, Canada.

'[When I was About Ten in Greenock]': Undated manuscript draft. W.S. Graham Estate archive.

W.S. Graham Bibliography

Books by W.S. Graham

Cage Without Grievance (Parton Press, 1942)
The Seven Journeys (William MacClellan, 1944)
2ND Poems (Poetry London Editions, 1945)
The White Threshold (Faber and Faber, 1949)
The Nightfishing (Faber and Faber, 1955)
Penguin Modern Poets 17 (with David Gascoyne and Kathleen Raine) (Penguin, 1970)
Malcolm Mooney's Land (Faber and Faber, 1970)
Implements in Their Places (Faber and Faber, 1977)
Collected Poems (Faber and Faber, 1979)
Selected Poems (ECCO Press, New York, 1980)
Uncollected Poems (Greville Press, 1990)
Aimed at Nobody: Poems from Notebooks, edited by Margaret Blackwood and
    Robin Skelton (Faber and Faber, 1993)
Selected Poems (Faber and Faber, 1996)
The Nightfisherman: Selected Letters of W.S. Graham, edited by Michael and
    Margaret Snow (Carcanet Press, 1999)
New Collected Poems, edited by Matthew Francis (Faber and Faber, 2004)
Approaches to How They Behave (Donut Press, 2009)
Les Dialogues obscurs: Selected Poems in French, translated by Anne-Sylvie Homassel
    and Blandine Longre (Black Herald Press, 2013)

Key Books on W.S. Graham

Give Me Your Painting Hand: W.S. Graham & Cornwall, by David Whittaker
    (Wavestone Press, 2015)
The Constructed Space: A Celebration of W.S. Graham, edited by Jonathan Davidson
    and Ronnie Duncan (Jackson's Arm, 1994)
The Poetry of W.S. Graham, by Tony Lopez (Edinburgh University Press, 1989)
Where the People Are: Language and Community in the Poetry of W.S. Graham,
    by Matthew Francis (Salt Publishing, 2004)
W.S. Graham: Speaking Towards You, edited by Ralph Pite and Hester Jones
    (Liverpool University Press, 2004)

Key Journals

Aquarius 25/26: George Barker/W.S. Graham (2002)
Edinburgh Review #75: The Life & Works of W.S. Graham (1987)
Journal of British and Irish Innovative Poetry, Volume 4, Number 1 (March 2012)
Poetry (January 2018)